Traveling the World
Through Your Favorite Movies

FILM+TRAVEL

EUROPE

MUSEYON
GUIDES

A CURATED GUIDE TO YOUR OBSESSIONS

www.museyon.com

© Museyon, Inc. 2009

Publisher: Akira Chiba
Editor-in-Chief: Anne Ishii
Art Director: Alene Jackson
Production Manager: Michael Yong
Photography Editor: Michael Kuhle
Film Stills: Courtesy of Everett Collection

Permission to use "La Dolce Vita" courtesy of: © International Media Films, Inc.
Cover Illustration: © Jillian Tamaki copyright 2008

Published in the United States by:
Museyon, Inc.
20 E. 46th St. Ste. 1400
New York, NY 10017

Museyon is a registered trademark.
Visit us online at www.museyon.com

ISBN 978-0-9822320-0-2

021059

Printed in China

GREENLAND

ICELAND

SWEDEN

NORWAY

FINLAND

RUSSIA

DENMARK

BELGIUM

UK

GERMANY

FRANCE

SPAIN

ITALY

TURKEY

MAP : **EUROPE**

TABLE OF CONTENTS

01 : LANDSCAPES OF IMAGINATION: CINEMATIC LEGACY — 09

SPAIN BY SHARI KIZIRIAN

02 : BEYOND BAGUETTES — 31

FRANCE BY JULIEN SEVEON

03 : STREET WALKING — 49

ITALY BY LIZ BROWN

TABLE OF CONTENTS

08 : FROM RUSSIA, WITH LUXE 139
RUSSIA BY LAUREL MAURY

READING / VIEWING 157
APPENDIX

INDEX + CREDITS 159
FILM

FOREWORD

I hate being labeled a tourist. The word brings to mind tour buses and large groups of strangers clogging up roadways and obscuring views.

Don't get me wrong, I'm sure we've all gone sightseeing and visited those 'must-see places' recommended by even the most general of guidebooks. Those 'must-see places' have an importance and are well-worth seeing, but there is something uniquely exhilarating about diverging from the beaten path to make your own 'discoveries.' It is those 'discoveries' that we remember most.

Our thirst for knowledge and interest in other places and peoples often takes us into uncharted territory. The Museion, built in ancient Alexandria, Egypt, was an institute founded to expand our knowledge and dedicated to the Muses, the sister goddesses of art, poetry, literature, philosophy and music. The Museyon Guides were created as an expression of that same endeavour. Unique in their format, the Museyon Guides are written for those who are ready to detour and experience culture through their own interests and obsessions.

The first of the Museyon Guides, *The Museyon Guide: Film+Travel*, takes off across Europe discovering those picture-perfect scenes from movies we all know and love. Visit Sergio Leone's wild west in Andalusia, Spain, or head to the Gulf of Naples and the island of Procida to discover the post office in *Il Postino*. By taking the leap to travel to these destinations we discover that the backdrop of these films provides a gateway into a country and culture that is often overlooked.

Meticulously researched from every angle by film reviewers, producers, directors and location specialists, Museyon will transform your relationship with film and change the way you travel.

I hope to see you on location.

01

LANDSCAPES OF IMAGINATION: CINEMATIC LEGACY

SPAIN

SHARI KIZIRIAN
Most memorable experience in film/travel: Watching *Octopussy*, starring an over-the-hill Roger Moore and the scantily clad Maud Adams, in a gender-segregated movie theater in downtown Cairo.

Galicia •

Navarre •

Cap de Creus •

• Segovia

Catalonia •

Ávila •

• Soria

• Barcelona

Madrid •

Esquivias •

• Peñiscola

Extremadura •

• Denia

Guadix •

• Tabernas

Cadiz •

Alméria •

A typical trip to Spain

entails boarding a train in France to cross the Pyrenees and taking a city-dotted tour of well-worn cultural hotspots. Barcelona's dizzying Sagrada Familia, Madrid's Prado museum, and the Moorish architecture of Seville are de rigueur, with perhaps a jaunt north to San Sebastian's old city in quaint, seaside Basque country and a possible stopover in Pamplona, bulls or no. Then it's back to Paris for the return flight home.

While a fine itinerary, this plan rushes through much of what makes Spain Spanish. From the rocky green Pyrenees to the spiky mountains of Extremadura, to the parched plains of La Mancha, which fired the imagination of Cervantes's Don Quixote, and the undulating deserts of Andalusia, Spain offers a remarkable and varied geography. Often only glimpsed by passengers through a moving train's windows, these landscapes are familiar to anyone with an interest in cinema. They just might not know they were looking at Spain.

Long shots of the taciturn, poncho-draped Clint Eastwood facing down danger in unforgiving terrain are perhaps the most enduring images of the American West. Yet they were filmed in Spain's southern province of Andalusia. Sergio Leone's famed spaghetti western trilogy (*A Fistful of Dollars*, *For a Few Dollars More*, and *The Good, the Bad and the Ugly*) was shot in and around the arid **Desierto de Tabernas**, laced by the **Sierra de Los Filabres** and by the beaches of the **Costa del Sol**. The famous circular duel in *For a Few Dollars More* (and in Leone's *Once Upon a Time in the West*) was shot near **Los Albaricoques** (meaning apricots), a town offering easy access to the well-maintained coastal preserve of Cabo de Gata. **Cortijo Los Frailes** in Cabo de Gata played the monastery where Tuco's brother nurses Blondie back to health in *The Good the Bad and the Ugly*. While Tuco taunted the

recovering Blondie to give up the name on the grave that holds a fortune, the windows of the Los Frailes revealed one of the few verdant landscapes photographed in the trilogy: the **Cabo de Gata Natural Park**, a temporary Eden for the pair's uneasy truce.

Many other spaghetti westerns were shot in Andalusia in the 1960s and early '70s, thanks to a sunny, temperate climate suitable for year-round filming. British filmmaker Alex Cox returned to the region in the late '80s for *Straight to Hell*, his punk spoof of the genre. He filmed in the same badlands at **Guadix** and Tabernas as the Italian directors and camped out in Almería, at the Gran Hotel, where Leone villain Lee Van Cleef (Angel Eyes) had to be escorted from the bar.

The first Hollywood director to film extensively in Andalusia was David Lean. He had intended to film all the desert sequences for *Lawrence of Arabia* (1962) in Jordan, but cash-flow problems forced the producers to move the shoot to Spain. Lean sent second-unit director André de Toth (an accomplished director of films noir) in search of replacement landscapes. He found what he was looking for in the sleepy fishing village of **Almería**, and the film went on to create iconic images out of the surrounding deserts, including the famous silhouette shot of Peter O'Toole as Lawrence, arms outstretched in victory atop a vanquished Ottoman train. Still, the terrain was not quite to Lean's liking, so tons of yellow sand were brought in to "dress" the sets and a grove of palm trees was planted along the **Rambla de Tabernas**, the dry bed of a desert river. (Dubbed "**El Oasis**" by locals, it was reused in Leone's *For a Few Dollars More*.) Aqaba, the destination of Lawrence's first campaign in the movie, is played by the beach at **El Algarrobico**, near Carboneros, where a monstrous new hotel is now the target of protests by environmentalists.

American director Terry Gilliam later staged the battle against the Turks for *The Adventures of Baron Munchausen* along Almeria's coast. During an interview about the 1988 film, he remembered that while building supports for an attack tower, which kept sinking deep into the sand, the crew uncovered a mass grave from Spain's Civil War.

The victor in that war, dictator Francisco Franco, had been luring Hollywood's cash-conscious producers to the country long before Lean

and Gilliam. Behind the times both economically and politically as far as Western Europe was concerned, mid-century Spain offered what few other places could: a wide range of landscapes, from mountains to seasides and deserts; more than 2,000 castles and a plethora of ruins from the times of Romans, Visigoths, and Moors; and a government willing to divert legions of its army for long periods to serve as extras and set-building muscle. Areas of Andalusia, in particular Málaga and Almería, the last to surrender to Franco's Falange, offered miles and miles of unmarred vistas. The local governments had been denied development funds as punishment for their rebellion—and as a result these areas were attractive to producers with period scripts to film.

Robert Rossen shot at the 15th-century castle **Manzanares el Real** for his 1956 film *Alexander the Great*, the first of the Hollywood directors to do so officially under Franco's Operación Propaganda Exterior, the Generalissimo's attempt to bolster the image of Spain abroad. King Vidor recreated Biblical times in Saragossa and Madrid for *Solomon and Sheba* (1959). Stanley Kramer tells of Spanish resistance to Napoleon in *The*

Pride and the Passion (1956), a story for which Spain got to play itself. For the climactic scene, *guerrilleros* breach the medieval wall at **Ávila**, with its 88 lookout towers and nine gates. Built beginning in 1090, the wall is three meters thick and was designed to keep out both invaders and disease. Franco's army accommodated Kramer's star-studded shoot (which included Cary Grant, Sophia Loren, and Frank Sinatra) by simply tearing down telephone and electrical wires that obstructed the camera's view. Ten years later Orson Welles shot *Chimes at Midnight*, his 1965 film about the Shakespearean character Sir John Falstaff, at these same walls. No stranger to Spain, Welles spent time in Seville in the mid-'30s and later showcased **Alcázar de Segovia** in his low-budget murder mystery *Mr. Arkadin* (1955). Looming high in the background, that castle plays home to the elusive main character, whose ill-gotten riches corrupt those around him. (It's also believed to be

---

∧ ***The Pride and the Passion,*** 1957. photo: ©Stanley Kramer Productions/Everett Collection
➤ **Manzanares el Real** photo: ©Elena Aliaga

the inspiration for the queen's castle in Disney's 1937 animated feature *Snow White and the Seven Dwarfs*.)

The innovative producer Samuel Bronston reaped big rewards from the Ministry of Information and Tourism's coordinated effort to draw both producers and tourists to Spain. He shot *John Paul Jones* (1959) on Spain's **Costa Blanca**, in **Denia**, and built a studio 30 miles outside Madrid, commissioning scripts that would showcase vistas of other travel-worthy parts of Spain. His most successful production, *El Cid* (1961), starring Sophia Loren and Charlton Heston, tells the story of Rodrigo Díaz de Vivar, the Spanish national hero who wrested control of Valencia from the Moors in the 11th century. Director Anthony Mann used the 15th-century **Belmonte Castle** outside Cuenca as the 11th-century city of Calahorra and the old city of **Peñiscola,** on the **Costa Dorada,** stood in for Valencia. The pine forests of the Guadarrama mountains served for the stunning exterior shots.

The **Sierra de Guadarrama**, with easy access to Madrid, also doubled for the Danube River frontier where Emperor Marcus Aurelius promised a Pax Romana

ALMODOVAR'S MADRID

Pedro Almodovar is a man of recurring themes and fixations representing a point of view purely, if not typically, Spanish. In Spanish they call it "fixed iconography" and it is easily seen in the theme of *woman*, beginning with his own mother in *All About My Mother*. Delightful protagonists like Carmen Maura and Penelope Cruz are all venerated and have won numerous prizes and nominations including Cruz's 2007 Oscar nomination, for Best Actress. The list is so long that they have coined the term "Almodovar Girls" where Marisa Paredes, Rossi de Palma, Victoria Abril, Bibiana Fernandez, Maria Barranco, Monica Forque, Chus Lampreave, and other muses rest in the film director's own private Parnassus.

After interesting and attractive 3-dimensional women, the city of Madrid itself is Almodavar's second most obvious theme, having given rise to the phrase, "New York has Woody Allen. Rome had Fellini and Madrid is synonymous with Pedro Almodovar."

Some highlights in Almodovar's Madrid:

Villa Rosa
Villa Rosa bar in the Plaza Santa Ana is the location of the most famous scene shot with Miguel Bosé in Almodovar's 1991 film *High Heels*. Today the bar is a great place to have a tapa, listen to flamenco-influenced pop music and enjoy the tiled murals depicting pastoral scenes from Andalucia on the façade. Indoors there are Mudejar-influenced architectural features to treat the eye too, along with the ears and the stomach.

Café del Círculo de Bellas Artes
On the ground floor of the prestigious

‹ [top] **Peñiscola beach** photo: ©Pex Cornel
[bottom] **Belmonte Castle** photo: ©Matt Trommer

19

cultural center, this restaurant/bar/terrace overlooking the Calle Alcalá is haughty 1920s and decked out in soaring pillars, statues and grandiose chandeliers. Popular with Madrid's "artistic types" its restaurant was used in Almodovar's 1993 critique of the media, *Kika*. Here is where Victoria Abril and Peter Coyote meet to discuss a script and is still a great place to people watch while you have a fixed-price luncheon or a drink and a tapa.

Museo del Jamón
Almodovar filmed the end of *Live Flesh* on Arenal Street, taking advantage of the street decorations. One of the shots focused on the "Museo del Jamón" bar, a Madrid chain specializing in Spanish ham. The director filmed pedestrians along with some extras he had hired for the occasion from inside a van, incognito, letting the camera roll for hours.

Segovia Aqueduct, Plaza Mayor, Puerta de Alcalá
When Almodovar uses tourist attractions in his films they are portrayed in a surreal light. In *Matador* (1985), the high-rising and potentially dangerous Segovia Aqueduct is the dark, brooding backdrop to a Madrileño couple's obsessions. The night traveling scene over the Puerta de Alcalá was used as a background for the opening titles of *Live Flesh* and the Plaza Mayor is where Juan Echanove dances in solitude in one of the most delightful scenes from *The Flower of My Secret*. In the Plaza Mayor, the calamar bars on any of the plaza's side entrances should not be missed. These bars serve "bocatas de calamares" (lightly fried squid-ring sandwiches on buns), with beer or a glass of apple cider for only a couple of euros.

(Courtesy of Jill Arcaro-Gordon, Managing Director of Bestprograms.com in Madrid, Spain.)

to the Germanic barbarians in the Bronston-produced *The Fall of the Roman Empire* (1964). The day before principal photography began, director Anthony Mann wished for snow. He got his wish when the region's first snowstorm in 50 years hit on day one of shooting. The following year, David Lean would use the chilly area further north in **Soria** to build the ice palace where Doctor Zhivago and his beloved Lara took final refuge from the Russian revolution. He too had hoped for snow, but ended up using white marble dust instead.

Spanish filmmakers have always made use of the landscapes at hand as well. In 1932 Luis Buñuel made his only documentary, *Las Hurdes (Land Without Bread)*, in the mountains of the autonomous community of **Extremadura**, on the Portuguese border. During the two-month shoot, Buñuel

^ *All About My Mother*, 1999. photo: ©Sony Pictures Classics/Everett Collection
≻ **Museo del Jamon** photo: ©zoonabar
[next page] **Las Cortes, Madrid** photo: ©Rafael Ramirez Lee

stayed in the hospitable village below in **La Alberca**. He bunked at the monastery **Las Batuecas**, calling it the closest place to paradise on earth, adding, however, that "the mountains were like infernos." Franco favored this area, where the conquistadors Cortés and Pizzaro were born, and today the mountains house quaint hillside hamlets and hiking trails along steep gorges and crystal clear streams.

Carlos Saura used the small village of **Esquivias**, where Cervantes married his wife Catalina, and the bleak scrublands of Seseña, Toledo, for his 1966 film *La Caza (The Hunt)*, about a hunting trip gone terribly awry. For *Cria Cuervos* (1976), which featured Geraldine Chaplin, his wife at the time, he shot at an estate in Madrid that he could see from his office window. In **Hoyuelos**, on the Castilian plains near Segovia, Victor Erice shot *The Spirit of the Beehive* (1973), about a contemplative young girl who, after her first encounter with cinema, becomes entranced by the possibility of a Frankenstein come to life. Spying a wounded rebel soldier across the ochre wheat field near her home, she braves a return visit to feed her newfound friend. Set in the 1940s, the masterfully photographed film captured the timelessness

of this remote Castilian village, which itself experienced movies for the first time when the film crew arrived for production in the mid-'70s.

Albert Lewin's *Pandora and the Flying Dutchman* is set in the fictitious coastal town of Esperanza. **Tossa de Mar** on Spain's **Costa Brava** in Cataluña, which extends from Barcelona to the French border, provided the actual location. Tossa de Mar features a scalloped edge of cove-protected beaches, watched over by the towers of the medieval fortifications of the **Vila Vela**, widely featured in the 1951 British film. A statue of Ava

Gardner, the female lead, now adorns the **Platja Gran**. The Catalan coast, of course, has a rich cinematic pedigree. Salvador Dalí hailed from **Cadaqués**, where he and Luis Buñuel later created the script for *L'Age d'Or*, Spain's first talking picture and a surrealist masterpiece. The action in *L'Age d'Or* begins at **Cabo de Creus**, where four bishops, dubbed "Majorcans," sit perched in full ecclesiastical regalia. Forty years later, Kirk Douglas would scramble over these same rocks to escape badass pirate Yul Brynner in *Lighthouse at the Edge of the World* (1971). Cabo de Creus, in this case, was a stand-in for Tierra del Fuego, whose winds are much fiercer than the *tramontana* that sweep down from the Pyrenees to create windsurfing-worthy seas.

More recent films showcase Spain's less-trod coasts to the north. **Llanes**, part of what is called **España Verde**, hosted the cast and crew of *The Orphanage* in 2006. The tree-covered cliffs hide a network of surf-washed grottos along **Bay of Biscay**; director Juan Antonio Bayona used one such cave, which becomes submerged at high tide, to spooky effect. On the Atlantic coast of **Galicia**, the most northeastern point of Spain, Alejandro Amenábar filmed the 2004 biopic *The Sea Inside*. He shot at **Playa das Furnas**, where the real-life Ramón Sampedro had his actual diving accident. Don't be fooled by the seaside sequence at the very beginning of the film—that palm-lined beach is in the Seychelles.

Geographic sleight-of-hand has been commonplace since cinema's beginnings, so deciphering the geography of films can be tricky. **Belchite**

is a town near Saragossa along the Pyrenees that was pummeled by Franco and its ruins left standing as a warning to rebels. In Guillermo del Toro's *Pan's Labyrinth* (2006), the **San Martín de Tours** at Belchite sits in mossy pine forests on the way to the Sierra de Guadarrama. Terry Gilliam set these same church ruins on a beach in Andalusia for *The Adventures of Baron Munchausen*.

With or without the intervention of CGI, Spain's unusual topography has served the wildest of imaginations. In *Conan the Barbarian* (1982), Spain

doubles for a fantastical prehistoric Europe, with **La Cuidad Encantada**'s unlikely mushroom-shaped rock protrusions as the setting for the home of a blood-sucking witch. (They had also appeared years before in *The Pride and the Passion*.) Terry Gilliam returned to Spain once more in 2000 to shoot *The Man Who Killed Don Quixote*. Production was a disaster from

the first day of shooting, and after a few weeks the producers ran out of money. Luckily, Keith Fulton and Louis Pepe's 2002 documentary *Lost in La Mancha* witnesses the production's unraveling and includes the doomed film's only completed scenes, shot at the **Bardenas Reales Nature Preserve**. Actually located in Navarra, its pleated, arid crags of limestone and clay seem otherworldly.

Still, the flat plains of Castile-La Mancha remain the psychological heart of Spain. Perhaps more than any other region, they represent a foreigner's conception of the country. It was here that Miguel de Cervantes, while imprisoned in **Argamasilla de Alba**, created Spain's most famous progeny, the demented and chivalrous knight who did battle with windmills. Pedro Almodóvar was born in La Mancha, in **Calzada de Calatrava**, Cuidad Real. Perhaps the most well-known of contemporary Spanish filmmakers, Almodóvar once attempted to explain how baroque creations such as Don Quixote can have come from La Mancha's desolate landscape. "It's just earth and the horizon, directly connected to the sky," he said. "It's almost abstract." Artists, he speculated, fill it with their rich imaginations. Travelers, whether drawn to these plains, the mountains, the seasides, or the cities of Spain, are welcome to do the same. §

The former editor of *Film Arts* magazine, Shari Kizirian has written extensively on the business and history of cinema. Her articles have been published by the San Francisco Silent Film Festival, the National Alliance for Media Arts and Culture (NAMAC), the Sundance Institute, and the International Documentary Association, among others. She currently lives in Rio de Janeiro, Brazil.

^ *Lost In La Mancha,* 2002. photo: ©Quixote Films/Everett Collection
‹ **Bardenas Reales Nature Preserve** photo: ©Eric Isselée

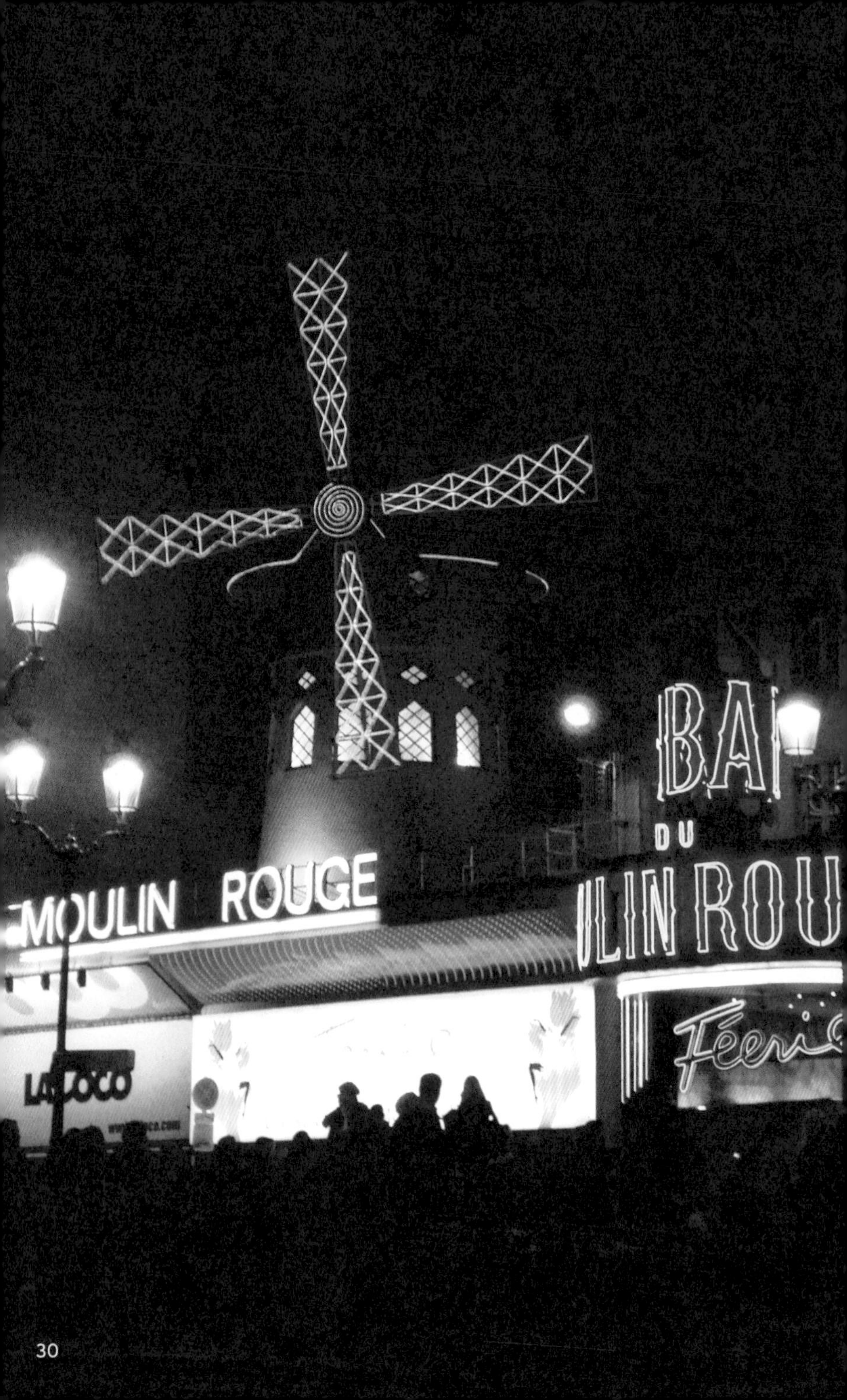
MOULIN ROUGE
BA
DU
LIN ROU

02

BEYOND BAGUETTES
FRANCE

JULIEN SÉVÉON
Most memorable travel experience: First time in Hong Kong.
Most memorable movie experience: Too many, so the latest,
Let the Right One In.

Baguettes, red wine, berets—to foreign eyes, France may seem like a simple, homogenous nation. In reality, between the Alsacians, the Basques, the Britons, the Corsicans and the Occitans, it's home to swaths of diverse regional languages, cultures, and architectural styles. And there's no better measure of its sundry geographical and social landscapes than in this Gallic nation's dynamic cinematic history.

BRITTANY

We start with Brittany, which lies at the country's western most tip. It was named after the Celtic Britons who inhabited the area autonomously prior to its annexation in 1532, and the nationalist French government has gone to great lengths over the years to suppress the region's language and influences, still seen in its sculpture-laden parishes. Most people outside of Brittany don't know much about the region, save the lush,

sweeping landscapes and dramatic, rocky coastlines that seem to seduce filmmakers. One of the most prodigious documentarians of the region: Claude Chabrol, the New Wave director who set 1969's *Que la Bête Meurt* (*This Man Must Die*) there, in **Quimper**—a cobblestoned, medieval hamlet abundant in 16th-century homes, whose almost Gothic atmosphere befitted the brooding picture. Chabrol would continue to shoot a string of movies in Brittany, including 1970's *Le Boucher* (*The Butcher*), 1977's *Alice ou la Dernière Fugue* (*Alice or the Last Escapade*) and 1990's *Jours Tranquilles à Clichy* (*Quiet Days in Clichy*).

Nearby you'll find the much more famous **Pont Aven**—home to the **Pont-Aven School of Art**, founded by post-impressionist artist Paul Gauguin. Nestled in a small valley on the border of the Aven River, this City of

---

^ **Claude Chabrol** photo: Keystone/Eyedea/Everett Collection
< **Medieval street, Brittany** photo: ©Paenen Gert
[previous page] **Pigalle at night** photo ©Ricardo Martins

58 FESTIVAL DE CANNES

PORTES 1. 2. 5. 6   ORCHESTRE PORTES 1. 2. 5. 6   PORTES 1. 2. 5. 6

Painters lives up to its wistful nickname—largely due to its proximity to the Forest of Love, a verdant locale that sits at the town's perimeter. Oddly enough, no Gauguin biopics have actually been shot here, but two comedies have: 1975's *Les Galettes de Pont-Aven* (*The Cookies of Pont-Aven*) and 1983's *Un Chien dans un Jeu de Quilles* (*A Dog in a Game of Nine-Pins*), the latter starring French comedy legend Pierre Richard. Both films made extensive use of Pont Aven as well as other small surrounding cities, notably the charming, tiny harbor town of **Doëlan**, located in a quiet loch. New Waver Eric Rohmer, meanwhile, found inspiration in another seaside town for 1996's *Conte d'Eté* (*A Summer's Tale*), the warm, sun-kissed third installment in his *Four Seasons* quartet of films. His movie takes place in the resort of **Dinard**, where no less than 407 charming villas date back to the Belle Epoque period.

L'OCCITANIE

Though it's not a state per se, L'Occitanie does refer to a very large region in the south of France that includes the certifiably fabulous cities of Toulouse, Marseille, and Saint Tropez. During the past 50 years or so, the area has been attracting wealthy international guests, notably Angelina Jolie and Brad Pitt, who recently settled there for a bit amid their never-ending world tour. **Saint Tropez** is arguably the most popular point on the Côte d'Azur (or Azure Coast, in the French Riviera), a hotspot characterized by easy living and lingering vacations, especially among the country's film community in the '50s. Jean Girault further stoked this reputation with his 1964 comedy *Le Gendarme de St. Tropez* (*The Gendarme of Saint Tropez*), the first in his very successful series of movies showcasing the town.

Though the larger city of **Marseille**—located some 68 miles from St. Tropez—doesn't boast the same jet-setting appeal as St. Tropez, it has been immortalized in hundreds of film productions. Cineaste Marcel Pagnol most memorably spotlighted the city in his "Fanny Trilogy." Those

^ *A Summer's Tale,* 1996. photo: ©Les Films du Losange/Everett Collection

‹ [top] **St. Tropez** photo: ©Elena Elisseva

[bottom] **Evening, Cannes Film Festival** photo: ©Vinicious Tupinamba

[next page] **Marseille** photo: ©Peeter Viisimaa

films—*Marius* (1931), *Fanny* (1932) and *César* (1936)—depicted the place as a lively, sometimes boisterious, destination. However, Marseille is best known internationally as a bastion of crime—especially in the heroin trade—thanks to William Friedkin's *French Connection* (1971) and its sequel four years later, directed by John Frankenheimer. Despite this unsavory reputation, Friedkin captured the beauty of Marseille in his movie, and did not miss his chance to shoot in the **Le Panier** district that's filled with cramped streets and colorful homes. Frankenheimer followed his predecessor's lead, ending *French Connection II* with an impressive car chase at the picturesque **Old Port**—one of Marseille's main attractions that barely survived a Nazi invasion at the end of World War II.

Need an excursion? It'll take you a few hours to travel from Marseille to **Corsica**, known as the island of beauty. Just like Brittany, Corsica used to be an independent state, and its indigenous population has managed to preserve its Mediterranean culture, despite a significant decline in use of the native tongue since the beginning of the 20th century. Think of Corsica as a small getaway, offering nature lovers numerous beaches and a clear warm sea, as well as mountains and forests. Philippe Harel explored the Corsican terrain for his 1997 film, *Les Randonneurs* (*Hikers*), which follows a group of Parisians who trek through the stunning isle.

PARIS
Of all the Gallic cities, none is more stereotypically French than Paris, which explains why it's long been a favorite of tourists and filmmakers alike. There have been a number of big-screen interpretations of Victor Hugo's *The Hunchback of Notre Dame*, so we'll just name-check one of the most famous ones: the 1923 version starring Lon Chaney as Quasimodo. You can find the **Cathédrale Notre Dame de Paris**, the imposing Gothic monument ornamented with flying buttresses and

^ *French Connection,* 1971. photo: ©20th Century Fox/Everett Collection
> **Bonifacio, Corsica** photo: ©Randi Utnes

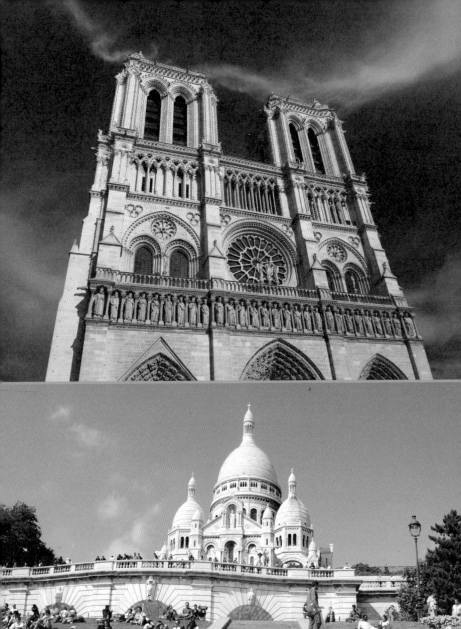

innumerable gargoyles, on the Île de la Cité.

In the northwest part of town, the elevated **Butte Montmartre** neighborhood (it sits on a hill) gained attention after the release of 2001's puckish romance *Amelie*. As such, some visitors may be a bit disappointed to find the neighborhood more modern

than the film would suggest. That said, Montmartre—previously the preferred bohemian digs of such seminal artists as Dalí, Renoir, Monet, Picasso, and Van Gogh—possesses an incredible view of Paris from the Basilica of the Sacré Coeur (especially at night with a clear sky).

But not all visions of Paris are romantic. Marcel Carmé shot his 1938 movie *Hotel du Nord* near the **Canal Saint Martin**

BELGIUM BY "IN BRUGES"

With unprecedented cooperation and support from Bruges—including from burgomaster (mayoral equivalent) Patrick Moenaert, and hundreds of locals working as extras—filming of Martin McDonagh's *In Bruges* captures the city as no other film has. While a couple of other projects, including one other major feature film (Fred Zinnemann's 1959 *The Nun's Story*, starring Audrey Hepburn), had shot on location in Bruges over the years, the *In Bruges* production was by far the most extensive to date.

When pressed to name a favorite location, McDonagh cites not one but three. He notes, "The boys' hotel was actually the same hotel I stayed in on my first trip, before I had any inkling I'd write something set in Bruges. I loved the market square, where most of the action takes place.

"But I also loved filming on the canals. It was such a beautiful blue-skied cold and misty morning. We scrambled to get rolling before the mist lifted, and I think we got some lovely stuff that day."

The production's nearly all-access pass meant that parts of Bruges will be revealed on-screen even to those familiar with the city. A particular standout—in all respects—is the **Bell Tower**, which looms 83 metres high (or, over 250 feet tall). 366 steps must be climbed to reach the pinnacle, where in the belfry one is then rewarded with a breathtaking view of all of Bruges and the surrounding countryside.

The film shoot within the film, was situated primarily outside the **Gruuthuse Museum** (which houses artifacts and objects spanning the 15th century to the 20th). This is not to be confused with the **Groeninge Museum**, where the cast and crew was allowed inside to film a conversation on purgatory.

The Groeninge showcases works by such legendary artists as Hieronymus Bosch, René Magritte, Jan van Eyck, among many others, and Colin Farrell and Brendan Gleeson found themselves happily occupied between takes strolling about the galleries.

Other locations included the '**Lake of Love**,' which used to be better known as Minnewater, a regular conduit between Bruges and Ghent, but is now more of a romantic rendezvous point; **Jan van Eyckplein Square**, by the **Spiegelrei canal**; the **Bruges train depot; Cafedraal restaurant**, where Ferrell's Ray takes Chloé out to dinner; **Diligente bar**, where Glesson's Ken drops in for a drink; and **Basilica of the Holy Blood**, where Ken waits on line, the chapel of which contains the famous Relic of the Holy Blood. Due to concerns over the Relic, the production did receive a rare turn-away, and was obliged to film in a different church nearby. The majority of the interiors – such as the homes of local arms dealer Yuri, and Chloë – are in fact in Bruges.

McDonagh plans to visit the city again, confiding, "I actually can't wait to go back to Bruges, but I think I'd better go before the film comes out there— 'cause they're probably gonna kill me."

(Courtesy of Focus Films Online)

(where Jean-Pierre Jeunet also filmed parts of *Amelie*) at the the eponymous inn, which has withstood a couple of proposed demolitions thanks to local protesters. This milestone of French cinema delivers a very touching view of the little people living there at the time. However, the area, which was still working class even a decade ago, has become a highly fashionable destination where the bo-bo (or bourgeois-bohême) spend their evenings sipping wine along the canal.

For a whirlwind tour of the City of Lights, turn to 2006's aptly named *Paris, Je t'aime* (or *Paris, I Love You*), an assortment of film shorts directed by 22 (!) different directors, ranging from Olivier Assayas to Wes Craven to Gus Van Sant. Most of the major attractions can be found in the film—the previously mentioned Montmatre, the red-light district of **Pigalle**, and the old, stately **Le Marais** quarter. But the movie

also traverses lesser-known spots such as the lovely **Faubourg Saint Denis** and the Paris Metro station at **la Place des Fêtes**. It'll be definitely worth your while to watch *Paris, Je t'aime* before exploring France's capital.

When you're done with the big city, take a quick jaunt out to the grandiose **Le Chateau de Versailles,** the crib that Louis XIII built that

was expanded by his successor, frequently referred to as Louis the Great or the Sun King. Popular classics like 1954's *Si Versailles m'était conté (Royal Affairs in Versailles)* and 1966's *Angélique et le Roy (Angelique and the King)* serve as veritable guided tours of the palace and its gardens. Great care has been taken over the centuries to preserve this edifice and its surroundings, which still appear as they did back in the 1600s when Louis XIV moved his court there. The only new addition: the common folk, who can now stroll around the royal residence where they once had no right to set foot. Bon voyage, indeed! §

Julien Sévéon is a Breton film critic living in Paris and writing about popular cinema from all parts of the world.

03

STREET
WALKING
ITALY

LIZ BROWN
Most memorable film/travel experience: I've certainly been the
innocent abroad, or less poetically, the American rube. I can
relate to such travelers as Daisy Miller and Lucy Honeychurch,
but I wish instead I could be a citizen of Rome and possess
a combination of Anna Magnani's swagger, Marcello Mastroi-
anni's cool, and Monica Vitti's mystique.

Milan

Venice

Pigneto

Florence

Rome

Procida · Napoli
Ischia

Sardinia

Matera

Palermo

Savoca

Sicily

Palazzo Adriano

Ragusa · Siracusa

Touring Italy by way of the movies. Where

to begin? Or more dauntingly, where to stop? Many popular
tourist spots, like the **Roman Forum**, will be already familiar to
filmgoers of all kinds. For those seeking to follow the path of
innocents abroad, you can visit the **Arch of Settimio Severo**.
It's here among the ruins that Gregory Peck and Audrey
Hepburn have their first run-in in William Wyler's romantic
comedy, *Roman Holiday* (1953). Other stops for the couple in
Rome include the **Trevi Fountain**, the **Spanish Steps (Piazza
di Spagni)**, and **Piazza del Popolo**, the very square where
River Phoenix as Mike, the narcoleptic prostitute in Gus Van
Sant's *My Own Private Idaho* (1991), wakes up at the base of
the **Egyptian obelisk of Ramses II**.

ROME IN A DAY

The Roman odyssey that takes 93 minutes in Vittorio De Sica's classic *The
Bicycle Thief* (1948) would be a grueling, zigzagging, near impossible day of

sightseeing for even the most intrepid film
pilgrim. It's certainly a bitter sojourn for poor
Antonio Ricci, who embarks upon a desperate
quest after a thief makes off with his bike.
Starting in the bustling city center, midway
between the Trevi and Tritone Fountains, you'll
find the **Traforo Umberto I**, the tunnel that
the perp first disappears into. Antonio and his
young son Bruno then head to the sprawling
Porta Portese flea market in the Trastevere,
a neighborhood on the west bank of the Tiber.
On Sundays visitors can still thread through
the mile-long spread of open-air booths and
secondhand finds where little Bruno puzzled
through horns and handlebars. Then, after a

sudden glimpse of the stolen bike at the **Porta Portese gateway,** Antonio
takes off on a frenzied sprint along the **Lungotevere**. Back on the other side
of the river, in the **Via Panico neighborhood**, he actually gets to confront
the thief, only to be outmatched by the man's angry neighbors. Finally, north

of the city, in view of the **Stadio Flaminio** at Via Pietro Da Contona No. 1, Antonio himself tries to steal a bike, a last, despairing act that fails in full view of his son.

PIGNETO

"Here they call 'em ruins. Back home we call 'em slums." So says Billy Dee Williams when he first gets to Rome. In *Mahogany* (1975), Williams is a political activist come to bring Diana Ross, a fashion designer, back from a life of unhinged decadence to her Chicago roots. Berry Gordy's only directorial effort is a delirious, rambling exercise in excess, a 1970s camp masterpiece of headpieces and scenery chewing in which Anthony Perkins' turn as a controlling, bitchy gay photographer almost upstages Ross's careening diva—but not quite.

Ross manages to take in a whirlwind tour of Rome's ruins, but neither she nor Williams make it east of the city to **Pigneto**, a neighborhood that well knew the literal meaning of the word. The working-class suburb, home to anti-Fascist resistance groups during the Nazi Occupation, was also the target of Allied bombing raids, and it was where Roberto Rossellini, Vittorio De Sica, and Pier Paolo Pasolini made a number of the films that are now classics of Italian neorealism.

Weeks after the liberation, Rossellini was out on the bombed-out streets shooting *Rome, Open City* (1945) with a cast that included non-actors who'd just lived through the very siege they were recreating. Just off Via Prenestina at **Via Montecuccoli No. 17** cinephiles can pay their respects at the spot where Anna Magnani's smoldering Pina is gunned down trying to rescue her fiancé from German troops.

Pasolini shot both *Accattone!* (1961) and *Mamma Roma* (1962), in Pigneto: the first a story of a pimp (Franco Citti) trying to lure a woman into prostitution and the second that of a woman (again Magnani) trying to leave prostitution to make a respectable life for her wayward son. Key stops: **Bar Necci** at Via Fanfulla da Lodi no. 68, a favorite haunt of both Accatone and Pasolini; the dome of **San Giovanni Bosco**, the church that bulges above **Cecafumo**, the blocky public housing complex where Mamma Roma lives; and **Parco degli Acquedotti**, the park where Magnani's son, the lanky, brooding Ettore (Ettore Garafalo) loses his virginity.

VATICAN CITY

Most films set in this sovereign city-state, such as *End of Days* (1999), *The Godfather, Part III* (1990), and *Hudson Hawk* (1991), have been shot on sets or in substituted locations. In the case of Ron Howard's *Angels & Demons* (2009), *The Da Vinci Code* (2006) prequel about a terrorist plot to destroy the Vatican, the Holy See not only rejected a request to shoot on the grounds but banned the "godless" production from working in any Catholic church. The filmmakers turned to the location that doubled for Vatican City in *Mission Impossible III* (2006), the **Caserta Palace** just north of Naples, and recreated the extensive grounds to scale in Los Angeles.

But the Vatican is in fact an active advocate for cinema. The Holy See has issued a list of what it considers great films, including *The Bicycle Thief*, Rossellini's *The Flowers of St. Francis* (1950), and Fellini's *La Strada* (1956) and *8 1/2* (1963). And in 1959 Pope John XXIII founded the **Vatican Film Library** to collect and preserve film and television programs related to the Catholic Church. There's a small movie theater and laboratory for film restoration as well as over 7,000 titles. The library is currently working on a project to study films from 1896 to today that explore the transcendent.

EUR

Benito Mussolini envisioned the **Esposizione Universale Roma**, a massive complex of sleek modern buildings and manicured knolls just south of the city center, as a monument to 20 years of Fascist rule. But construction of the EUR, begun in the 1930s, was brought to a halt by World War II. Work was subsequently resumed in the 1950s and 60s, and the resulting compound has provided the setting for many films. The resistance fighters in *Rome, Open City* (1945) stage an attack on the German police in front of the **Palazzo della Civiltà del Lavoro**. In *La Dolce Vita* (1960), Marcello takes his suicidal fiancée to the **Palazzo dei Congressi**, which doubles as the hospital. And it's this same building that serves as the office of the Fascist police in Bernardo Bertolucci's *The Conformist* (1979).

Michelangelo Antonioni explored modern alienation against the compound's austere landscape in *L'eclisse* (1962), the last film in the trilogy that includes *L'avventura* (1960) and *La Notte* (1961). Monica Vitti's watchful, doe-eyed translator first encounters stockbroker Alain Delon not in the futuristic district but on the floor of the **Borsa** (Rome's stock exchange), housed in the same structure as the Chamber of Commerce. Established in 1879 at

Piazza di Pietra, the building incorporates the ancient, remaining columns of **Hadrian's Temple** (145 AD). The characters' tentative romance, however, plays out predominantly on the EUR's barren streets. Vittoria's apartment is at **Viale dell' Umanesimo 307**, and a crucial early scene with her soon-to-be ex-lover takes place near the water tower, or **Fungo**, so-called for its mushroom-like shape.

FLORENCE

In Florence, you can retrace the steps of Lucy Honeychurch, the English heroine of E.M. Forster's *A Room with a View* (1985), as portrayed by Helena

Bonham Carter in the Merchant-Ivory film. Miss Honeychurch's aforementioned view-less room is at the Pensione Bertolini, which at the time of the filming was Quisisana e Ponte Vecchio, a hotel along the Arno that was damaged in 1993 by a bomb. However, the building has since been renovated and renamed the **Hotel degli Orafi**. You can follow in the footsteps of the anxious Charlotte Bartlett, Lucy's chaperone, who along with the lady novelist Eleanor Lavish (Judi Dench), takes in the statue of **Grand Duke Ferdinand** in Piazza Santissima Annunziata. Then there's Lucy's unescorted tour, which begins with the **monument to Dante at the Church of Santa Croce** and then continues to the **Piazza della Signoria** where she passes through the open-air museum at the entrance of the **Palazzo Vecchio**, a corridor of statues that includes Cellini's Perseus with the Head of Medusa, a copy of Michelangelo's David, and the Fountain of Neptune designed by Bartolomeo Ammannati.

VENICE

One of the most photogenic cities ever, Venice has been the setting for a number of globe-trotting film productions, such as Iain Softley's *The Wings of the Dove* (1997), Woody Allen's *Everybody Says I Love You* (1996), and *Casino Royale* (2006), Daniel Craig's first turn as James Bond. It is among the canals and alleyways that Donald Sutherland has his creepy premonitions in Nicolas Roeg's thriller *Don't Look Now* (1973). After the

^ *A Room with a View,* 1985. photo: ©Cinecom International/courtesy Everett Collection
‹ **Palazzo Vecchio, Florence** photo:'©Richmatts
[next page] **Venice canal** photo: ©Rostislav Glinsky

CINECITTÀ STUDIOS

Rome's legendary film studio was established in 1937 by Benito Mussolini, who declared, "Cinema è l'arma più forte" ("Cinema is the most powerful weapon"). Considered "Hollywood on the Tiber" during its heyday, Cinecittà was the site of such sword-and-sandal epics as *Quo Vadis* (1951), *Ben Hur* (1959), *Spartacus*

(1960), and the production and publicity disaster that was *Cleopatra* (1963). It was also, cinematically speaking, more home to Federico Fellini than the actual streets of Rome were. **Via Veneto** is featured prominently in *La Dolce Vita* (1960) as the paparazzi-crammed thoroughfare. And in **The Nights of Cabiria** (1957) it is on the same street that movie star Alberto Lazzari (Amedeo Nazzari) takes Cabiria out to a nightclub. But while Fellini included many other major landmarks, such as the **dome of St. Peter's**, in his films, he actually preferred filming in the studio, and his scenes of nightlife decadence and glamour were often shot on elaborately designed sets. In *Intervista* (1987), a documentary/tribute to the studio, Fellini describes Cinecittà as a fortress, or "maybe an alibi."

In the 1990s the studio was privatized and has since been closed to the public. Major features continue to be filmed and edited there, including *The Gangs of New York* (2002), *The Passion of the Christ* (2004), and *The Life Aquatic with Steve Zissou* (2004). Plans for a Cinecittà World, a kind of Universal Studios on the Tiber, are in the works.

death of his daughter, Sutherland comes to the city to work on the restoration of a church, **San Nicolo dei Mendicoli**, bordered by the Rio di San Nicolo and the Rio dell Terese. Although the graphic, improvised sex scene between Sutherland and Julie Christie takes place at the **Bauer Hotel** on Piazzo San Marco, Roeg used the façade and the lobby of the **Hotel Gabrielli Sandwirth** for the exterior shots.

In Luchino Visconti's *Death in Venice* (1971), Dirk Bogarde as the ailing Gustav von Aschenbach spends much of his time gazing at the beautiful Tadzio at the Lido beach. He stays at the lavish **Hotel des Bains**, which doubles in Anthony Minghella's *The English Patient* (1996) as the gathering place where all the diplomats and spies drink together in Cairo during the war. And in Sergio Leone's *Once Upon a Time in America* (1984), the epic story of Jewish gangsters living in New York's Lower East Side, Robert De Niro's Noodles takes his date out for dinner to an opulent Long Island joint, which was in fact the **Hotel Excelsior,** also on the Lido.

Minghella returned to Venice (as well as plenty of other Italian spots) for the filming of *The Talented Mr. Ripley* (1999). It is

^ **Ben Hur monument, Cinecittà Studios** photo: ©Akira Chiba
> **San Marco** photo: ©McPig

at the famed **Caffe Florian** on Piazzo San Marco that the elaborate ruse Matt Damon as Tom Ripley has set in motion begins to unravel when Gwyneth Paltrow as Madge becomes increasingly suspicious about Dickie Greenleaf's absence.

PROCIDA AND ISCHIA

Cinephiles with strong attachments to sun, sea and general leisure can indulge themselves in the Gulf of Naples. Just off the western coast of Italy in the Tyrrhenian Sea, the volcanic islands of Procida and Ischia provided Anthony Minghella with a movie-perfect "Mongibello," the fictional village where the scheming Tom Ripley first tracks down Dickie Greenleaf (Jude Law), the charismatic, wealthy wastrel, in *The Talented Mr. Ripley* (1999).

Castello Aragonese, a steep rocky fortress built in the 12th century, towers above the northeastern coast of Ischia, the larger of the two islands. Tom first alights in **Ischia Porto**, and it's also on Ischia, at **Bagno Antonio,** where Tom just happens to happen upon the sunbathing Dickie, who is staying nearby at an airy, white-walled villa, **Palazzo Malcovati**.

Less traveled than Ischia is Procida, home to the small fishing village of **Corricella**. It's through these small winding streets and among the pastel, terraced houses that the carefree Dickie rides his scooter, and at the top of Via San Rocco at the **Piazza dei Martiri** he makes his emphatic declaration to Tom that he will not return to America.

Minghella was not the only director to discover the cinematic delights of the small island. Michael Radford set much of *Il Postino* (1994) here, and the Piazza dei Martiri in particular is featured prominently, doubling as the location for the post office where Mario Ruoppolo (Massimo Troisi) comes to retrieve mail for the exiled Chilean poet Pablo Neruda (Philippe Noiret). After all the sun and sea, relax with a drink at **Bar La Taverna del Postino,** the very spot where Mario courts barmaid Beatrice (Maria Grazia Cucinotta).

∧ *Il Postino,* 1994. photo: ©Miramax/Everett Collection
‹ [top] **Castello Aragonese, Ischia** [bottom] **Corricella, Procida** photos: ©Akira Chiba

MATERA

In the city of Matera you can still get a sense of ancient history. Dug into the rocky hillside of the southern region of Basilicata, the "Sassi," caverns or houses, date back some 9,000 years. These rock-hewn settlements evoke a land out of time, and both Pier Paolo Pasolini and Mel Gibson have used this distinctive backdrop in their respective Bible stories, *The Gospel According to St. Matthew* (1964) and *The Passion of the Christ* (2004).

SICILY

Sicily, land of olives, artichokes and cannoli, has been the setting for a wide range of films: Roberto Rossolini's *Stromboli* (1950), Michelangelo Antonioni's *L'Avventura* (1960), Pietro Germi's *Divorce, Italian Style* (1961),

Luchino Visconti's *The Leopard* (1963), Luc Besson's *Le Grand Bleu* (1988), and Steven Soderbergh's *Ocean's Twelve* (2004). Francis Ford Coppola shot scenes from *The Godfather* (1972) not in the town of Corleone, though it exists, but in the smaller village of Savoca. There you can visit **Bar Vitelli** and the **Chiesa di Santa Lucia** where Michael (Al Pacino) marries Apollonia (Simonetta Stefanelli). In *The Godfather Part II* (1974), the scenes of Vito's early years are filmed in the nearby town of Forza d'Agro. Coppola returned to Sicily for *The Godfather Part III* (1990), this time to Palermo for the climactic scenes at the **Teatro Massimo**, the largest opera house in Italy and the site of Michael's final downfall.

Giuseppe Tornatore's Sicily, however, is a decidedly more heartwarming place. It's among the picturesque landscapes of **Ragusa** and **Siracusa** that the director set *The Star Maker* (1996) and *Malèna* (2000). Travelers can indulge their own movie nostalgia at the town of **Palazzo Adriano in Palermo** where Tornatore filmed the much-beloved *Nuovo Cinema Paradiso* (1988). §

Liz Brown has written about movies and movie stars for publications such as *Bookforum*, the *London Review of Books*, the *Los Angeles Times*, and the *New York Times Book Review*.

^ *Nuovo Cinema Paradiso*, 1989. photo: ©Miramax/Everett Collection
‹ [top] **Palazzo Adriano** [bottom] **Piazza Duomo, Siracusa** photos: ©Akira Chiba

04

INDULGE YOUR WANDERLUST
GERMANY

HANNAH TUCKER
Most memorable film/travel experience: As a red carpet reporter in New York City, I was constantly amazed by the realization that, in real life, most movie stars are really, really short.

Worried that a film-inspired tour of Germany
will feature nothing but bunkers and battlefields? Fear not. The land
of beer and bratwurst has overseen production on a wide range of
films, from the gloomy classic (*Nosferatu*) to the über-blockbuster
(*The Bourne Supremacy*). Start in the north and work your way
down to Bavaria, or take off from southerly Munich and trek up to
Hamburg. Just, whatever you do, make sure you hit Berlin.

BERLIN

Berlin's **Tempelhof Airport** would be the logical start to any cinematic tour
of the German capital. The foreboding main terminal—designed by Hitler's
architect Albert Speer—appears in *The Man Between* (1953), *Cabaret* (1972),
The Innocent (1993) and A *Foreign Affair* (1948), to name just a few famous
films. Unfortunately, Tempelhof was closed to air traffic in October 2008, but
the city has plans for what the head of Babelsberg film studios once called
"the mother of all airports." Soon, per some proposals, the building complex
will house a media center and old hangars will be converted into permanent
film sets.

Another iconic symbol of West Berlin, the **Zoologischer Garten** train
station is the site of a sabotaged CIA deal in Paul Greengrass's *The Bourne
Supremacy* (2004). Zoo and the surrounding area also symbolize the
temptation of capitalism in Georg Tressler's 1956 drama, *Teenage Wolfpack*.
And once you've been to the memorable Zoo, imposters are easy to spot
onscreen. Scenes at "Berlin Hauptbahnhof" in *Cabaret* (1972) and the 1992
melodrama *Shining Through* were filmed in Lübeck and Leipzig, respectively.

The nearby **Kaiser Wilhelm Memorial Church** makes an appearance in
the first minutes of Billy Wilder's 1961 comedy *One, Two, Three*, though its
haunting exterior is more suited to the cameo it makes in Wim Wenders'
Wings of Desire (1987). From the church take a stroll down **Kufürstendamm**,
the shopping boulevard Sean Connery (as James Bond) cruises down in
Octopussy (1983), en route to **Checkpoint Charlie** on Friedrichstraße, where
he is smuggled into the DDR. A replica of the guard stand is there (the
original is on display at the Allied Museum of Berlin-Zehlendorf), as well as
the Haus am Checkpoint Charlie museum, which chronicles some of the most
imaginative escapes in the other direction.

⟨ **Berlin** photo: ©seier+seier+seier
[previous page] **Oktoberfest, Munich** photo: ©Losevsky Pavel

Wings of Desire is as good as any guidebook when it comes to the sights of Western Berlin. In addition to the Kaiser Wilhelm Church, where Damiel is perched in the first scene, Wenders' moody drama takes viewers to the **Staatsbibliothek** (City Library) in the Tiergarten district, a gathering place for angels in the film. The **Siegersäule** (Victory Column) and **Potsdamer Platz** provide two of Damiel's haunts.

A grander former East-West checkpoint is the **Brandenburg Gate**, which towers in the background of *The Man Between and A Foreign Affair*. Lorelei, the smoky bar where Marlene Dietrich sings "Black Market" in the latter film was actually the **Femina Bar** on nearby Nürnberger Straße in the western district of Schöneberg. The building now houses the Ellington Hotel, which has a nostalgic "Femina" lounge.

In *One, Two, Three*, the first shot of the Brandenberg Gate coincides with MacNamara's comment, "Some of the East German police were rude and suspicious; some were suspicious and rude." In fact, Wilder was only permitted to film the majestic gate from the Western side. Everything in the "East" was shot on a set in Munich.

One, Two, Three also features an actual Berlin Coca-Cola plant. The building on Hildburghauser Straße was abandoned in 1992, though its weary exterior remains intact. The plant even had a cameo in 2003's *Good Bye Lenin!*, when protagonists Denis and Alex film part of a fake news broadcast in front of the building. Wolfgang Becker's dramedy was also shot on location on and around the imposing Karl-Marx-Allee, an enduring showcase of the DDR's love of cement. The tenement where Alex and his ailing mother live is on **Berolinastraße**, while a protest scene was filmed at the Underground station **Mohrenstraße**.

In *The Lives of Others* (2006), Ulrich Muhe plays an East German secret policeman assigned to spy on a playwright. At one point his character, Captain Wiesler, is walking down **Karl-Marx-Allee** as Dreyman, the playwright, follows him. The eponymous Karl Marx Bookstore whereWiesler finds Dreyman's book, closed in 2008, but the store's sign—like all of Karl-Marx-Allee—remains a protected landmark.

Just to the north is **Alexanderplatz**, an essential stop for any Berlin visitor. A shot of the public square's U-Bahn station is the opening scene in the Jodie Foster action flick *Flightplan* (2005). (What is supposed to be Berlin Tegel, however, is the less-ugly Leipzig-Halle airport.) The two most prominent

features of "Alex" are the 1,207-foot-tall (368 m) TV tower with its distinctive, candy-cane striped antenna, and the rotating World Time Clock. Jason Bourne (Matt Damon) meets Nicky (Julia Stiles) here in *The Bourne Supremacy*, but that's just one stop on Bourne's packed Berlin tour. He arrives in the capital at the Ostbahnhof train station and takes a cab ride over the ornate Oberbaum Bridge—which also pops up in *Run Lola Run* (1998). Later, Bourne evades the Polizei by jumping from a bridge over the **Spree River** at the **Friedrichstraße** station onto a conveniently placed boat

Bourne also showcases a few housing options for Berlin visitors. Villain Kirill (Karl Urban) swings by Motel Avus near the **Funkturm (radio tower)** in the west of the city, while Pamela Landy (Joan Allen) prefers to cool her heels at the five-star Westin Grand on Friedrichstraße, near **Unter den Linden**. (In *Run Lola Run* the title heroine runs through **Babelplatz**, the square across from **Humboldt University** on Unter den Linden. The square is notable for its underground memorial to the Nazi book burnings.)

Before moving on from Berlin, drag yourself out to the suburbs for a look at Frederick the Great's **Sanssouci** in Potsdam. The rose-colored **Neues Palais** became cinematographer Alcott's 18th-century Berlin in Stanley Kubrick's epic drama *Barry Lyndon* (1975). Potsdam is also home to the famous **Studio Babelsberg**, where hundreds of films, from Fritz Lang's *Metropolis* (1927) to James McTeigue's *V for Vendetta* (2006) were filmed. You can visit retired movie sets at the Filmpark Babelsberg.

HAMBURG

Wondering what to do in Hamburg? Why not begin with the James Bond tour? In *Tomorrow Never Dies* (1997), 007 (Pierce Brosnan) arrives at the Hamburg Fuhlsbüttel airport and meets up with Q (Desmond Llewelyn). Some of the parking garage car chase was shot here, but the penultimate sequence was filmed on the roof of the luxurious **Atlantic Hotel** on the Alster lake, and the car's final jump over the street and into a (fake) Avis car rental office happens on **Mönckebergstraße**, one of Hamburg's busiest shopping streets. The site of the crash is the **Galeria Kaufhof Department Store**. The front of the Atlantic Hotel also appears in *Tomorrow Never Dies*.

Wim Wenders' *The American Friend* (1977) casts Hamburg in a much different light, as Tom Ripley (Dennis Hopper) prowls **St. Pauli**, the neighborhood where the art dealer Zimmerman (Bruno Ganz) lives, as well as the harbor and the Old Elbtunnel, which emits an eerie glow undiminished today by the constant stream of tourists. (The 2002 remake, *Ripley's Game*, trades Hamburg for Berlin, with scenes filmed in the **Aquarium** and **Gendarmenmarkt** square.)

Darker still is director Fatih Akin's take on the port city in *Head-On* (2004). The club **Fabrik** in Hamburg-Altona is where the drug-addled Cahit (Biro Ünel) works washing glasses at the bar.

Further out to sea, Wolfgang Petersen's *Das Boot* (1981)—which was the most expensive German movie ever made until Tom Tykwer (the director of *Run Lola Run*) made *Perfume: The Story of a Murderer* in 2006—features scale models of U-boats in the North Sea. U-995, the last real submarine of the type recreated for the film, is on display at the **Laboe Naval Memorial** near Kiel.

For *Nosferatu* (1922), director J.W. Murnau made for Wismar, a port town on the Baltic Sea near Lübeck. The harbor, St. Mary's Church (of which only the tower remains) and the town square were among locations used for the classic silent film. Werner Herzog used much of the same Wismar scenery for his 1979 remake starring Klaus Kinski.

ELTVILLE AM RHEIN

Jean-Jacques Annaud's thriller about murderous men of the cloth, *The Name of the Rose* (1986), was largely filmed inside the **Eberbach Monastery** in Eltville am Rhein, Hessen. Though it is still called Kloster Eberbach, the place hasn't been a monastery since 1803. After that it served Eltville as a prison and a mental institution; today it is open to the public as a center for viniculture and the arts.

FRANKFURT

Two films show two very different sides of Frankfurt. *Diamonds are Forever* (1971) was filmed in the Lufthansa hangar at **Frankfurt International Airport**, one of the busiest airports in the world. In contrast, Jacques Tourneur focuses on the dismal, bomb-ruined streets of post-World-War-II Frankfurt in his black-and-white 1948 film, *Berlin Express*.

MAYEN

Bürresheim Castle, located northwest of Mayen in Western Germany, is perhaps better known by another name. In *Indiana Jones and the Last Crusade* (1989), the 12th-century palace is Castle Brunwald where Indy's father (Sean Connery) is held prisoner. The film relocates Bürresheim to the German-Austrian border, but it's actually closer to Belgium and Luxembourg.

NUREMBERG (NÜRNBERG)

The city of Nuremberg—the site of Nazi rallies under Hitler's regime and the Nuremberg Trials in 1945 and 1946—lies 105 miles (170km) north of Munich. The hearings took place at the Palace of Justice, at Fürther Strasse 110. Stanley Kramer later filmed *Judgement at Nuremberg*—a fictionalized account of the tribunal—here in 1960. In the outdoor scene when Judge Haywood (Spencer Tracy) buys a hot dog from a street vendor, he's standing on the **Hauptmarkt** with the **Church of our Lady** (Frauenkirche) in the background.

MUNICH

The city of Munich has provided fanciful background for several films. The game scenes in Norman Jewison's sci-fi *Rollerball* (1975), for example, were filmed in Munich's Olympic Basketball Arena. And when a crowd gathers to catch a glimpse of five golden ticket winners in *Willy Wonka and the Chocolate Factory* (1971), they're actually standing outside an **old gasworks building and clocktower on Emmy-Noether-Straße.**

---

^ *Indiana Jones And The Last Crusade*, 1989. photo: ©Paramount Pictures/Everett Collection
> **Castle Sanssouci, Potsdam** photo: ©extranoise

Outside the city no less than three castles were used to create one extravagant hotel in Alain Resnais' Last Year in *Marienbad* (1961). **Nymphenburg Palace**, the baroque summer home of Bavaria's late rulers, is only 20 minutes from the city center. The **Amalienburg**, Charles VII's rococo hunting lodge, is on the palace grounds. The third Marienbad castle is **New Schleissheim Palace**, which houses the famous gallery of baroque paintings, in the northwestern suburb of Oberschleißheim. New Schleissheim is also the French army's rather swank field headquarters and the site of the court martial in Stanley Kubrick's *Paths of Glory* (1957). Colonel Dax's headquarters is the **Old Schleissheim Palace**, which was badly damaged in World War II.

HOHENSCHWANGAU

The village of **Hohenschwangau**, in southwest Bavaria, is home to Ludwig II's **Palace Neuschwanstein**. The neoromantic castle has seen over 50 million tourists and quite a few Hollywood productions, including the Mel Brooks parody *Spaceballs* (1987) and *The Wonderful World of the Brothers Grimm* (1962). In *Chitty Chitty Bang Bang* (1968), Baron Bomburst (Gert Frobe) lives in Neuschwanstein (although only the exterior shots show the real castle). When Baroness Bomburst (Anna Quayle) is ejected from Chitty and falls into a lake, she's in Alpensee near the castle.

ROTHENBURG OB DER TAUBER

The picturesque medieval town where the Potts family live (and fly over) is Rothenburg ob der Tauber in Northwest Bavaria. From the air, Rothenburg also looks like the town Charlie and his Grandpa fly above in the glass elevator at the end of *Willy Wonka and the Chocolate Factory*. This scene, however, was actually shot in Nördlingen, which is south of Rothenburg.

If your Eurail pass is still valid, you could spend a day riding the rails between Hamburg and Munich (in an homage to *The Great Escape*, of course). Otherwise, it's time to bid goodbye to the Deutschland—though you might want to plan a trip back in a year or two. At the time of writing, Brad Pitt and Quentin Tarantino were finishing up *Inglourious Basterds* in Berlin, and Tom Cruise had wrapped *Valkyrie* after filming in Potsdam.

Hannah Tucker is a language consultant and freelance writer living in Hamburg, Germany. She has written about film and pop culture for *Entertainment Weekly* magazine.

‹ **Berlin alleyway** photo: ©Wolfgang Staudt

05

THE LOCAL ORIENT
ISTANBUL, TURKEY

PELIN TURGUT
Most memorable film/travel experience: Little beats the genuine enthusiasm and enchantment afoot in the ancient city of Kars, a sleepy ancient town in Eastern Turkey (famously depicted in Orhan Pamuk's novel *Snow*), when the Festival on Wheels stops there every November. Locals, few of whom speak a foreign language, brave snow and bitter cold to pack screenings of adventurous European films.

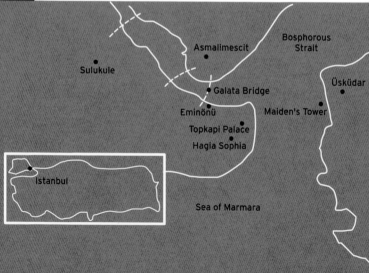

Few journeys evoke a bygone era of smoky
old world glamour and romance as dramatically as the Orient
Express, the fabled train which ran from Paris to Istanbul from
the turn of the 19th century onward. Its polished wood paneling
and brass fittings, Lalique glassware and champagne-swilling
glitterati were immortalized in the eponymous Agatha Christie
thriller, later made into a film starring a debonair Sean Connery
(*Murder On The Orient Express*, 1974).

The Express no longer exists, but steaming into Istanbul by train at
daybreak is still the most poetic of entrances to this 1,500-year-old city.
The tracks curl past fortified Byzantine city walls and Old City minarets,
running parallel to the turquoise blue waters of the Sea of Marmara.
Fishing boats chug back from dawn forays while creaky ferries transport
commuters between Europe and Asia, trailing seagulls in their wake.

Twenty-first century
denizens short on
time can sample the
atmosphere at the
Sirkeci train station,
built in 1890, the
journey's original
end-point. Built by
a Prussian, it's an
imposing example
of European Orientalist architecture that remains almost unchanged.
The Orient Express restaurant, by Track 1, still offers up starched white
tablecloths, high ceilings, wood floors, dusty elegance and an instant trip
back in time. Even better, at affordable prices.

Spread out across a hilly peninsula behind Sirkeci is **Topkapi Palace**,
which was the administrative heart of the Ottoman Empire for more than
400 years and the site of imperial intrigue, opulence and bloody power
struggles. Today the palace is a museum, home to richly woven textiles,
silk carpets, jewel-encrusted imperial objects, armor, weaponry and
manuscripts—artifacts from a once-mighty empire.

It was begun by Sultan Mehmet II (Mehmed the Conqueror) who took the city from the Byzantines in 1453. A small city unto itself, in its heyday, thousands of people from every corner of the empire—which stretched from the Balkans to Africa—were employed here. Fine art was taken seriously at the court. The most talented artists were commissioned to create imperial objects, many of which are housed here today.

Fans of the Oscar-winning 1964 film *Topkapi*, starring Peter Ustinov, can see the famous dagger, object of the movie's planned heist, here. Originally crafted in 1747 as a gift to the Persian King Nadir Shah, the dagger never made it to its recipient, who was killed in an uprising before the Ottoman emissary crossed the border into Iran. It features three unusually large emeralds in its handle, rows of diamonds and a mother-of-pearl covering.

Allow at least half a day to stroll through the kitchens, courtyards and ceremonial chambers, including the elaborate Harem.

A short walk away from the Palace brings you to the deluxe **Four Seasons Hotel**, converted—in an unlikely irony of fate—from the infamous former **Sultanahmet jail**, depicted in the Oscar-winning Alan Parker film *Midnight Express*. The controversial 1978 movie starred Billy Hayes as an American languishing in a nightmarish Turkish jail after being caught trying to smuggle drugs out of the country. It was in fact filmed almost entirely in Malta after Turkish officials denied permission to shoot in Istanbul.

Sultanahmet was the first jail to be built in Istanbul in 1918, designed in a neo-classical style that bears the stamp of nascent Turkish nationalism. Hundreds of intellectuals, writers and political dissidents were incarcerated in this four-story stone building organized around an open-air courtyard, including the great Turkish poet Nazim Hikmet. It was shut down in 1969, bought by the Four Seasons in 1992 and reopened as

an upscale hotel in 1996. Although hotel officials initially tried to downplay its jailhouse origins, they quickly found its history was a draw, though the hotel's swanky air make its past hard to believe. An overnight stay is pricey, but you can soak up the atmosphere over afternoon tea or Sunday brunch without breaking the bank.

On the other side of this historic peninsula, known as **Sultanahmet**, is the neighborhood of **Sulukule**, home to one of the world's oldest Roma

communities. Sorely neglected and on the brink of demolition, the district was once the pulsing heart of Istanbul's nightlife. Generations of residents passed through the area for music, drinking and belly dancing. It even played a small part in the 1963 James Bond film *From Russia with Love*, in which two curvaceous Roma dancers sweat it out to win the spy's favors. Today, the rundown neighborhood where the Roma still live communally, is threatened by the municipality's ambitious gentrification plans.

Bond, it seems, can't get enough of Istanbul. In 1999 the movie franchise returned to the city to film *The World is not Enough* in which the British spy unravels a scheme by bad guy Renard to disrupt oil shipments from the Caspian Sea by causing the meltdown of a nuclear submarine in the **Bosphorus** waterway.

The Bosphorus is the city's lifeline, dividing Europe from Asia and connecting the Black Sea to the Sea of Marmara. It is simultaneously inexorably modern—one of the world's busiest waterways, a controversial route for Russian oil tankers—and dreamy, an inspiration to writers, artists and filmmakers both Turkish and foreign.

One of the best ways to see the city is to take a $5 ferry from **Eminönü**, cruising past waterfront palaces, wood-framed Ottoman mansions and

^ *From Russia With Love,* 1963. photo: ©United Artists/Everett Collection
> **Istanbul alleyway** photo: ©Deniz Tavmen

swanky new nightclubs, disembarking to enjoy the catch of the day at one of the sleepy fishing villages at the mouth of the Black Sea.

Featured in the Bond film, the **Maiden's Tower** sits on a tiny islet just off the coast of Üsküdar. It's believed to date back to the days of ancient Greece when it served as a toll booth for passing ships. Popular legend holds that it was built by a sultan who sought to protect his beloved daughter against a prophecy that she would die of snakebite. He sequestered her away in a tower on the water and was her sole visitor. On her 18th birthday, he brought her a lavish basket of fruits to celebrate, whereupon a crafty snake hidden amongst the fruits emerged to bite the maiden. She subsequently died in her father's arms.

There is not much to see in the tower today although the cafe with panoramic Bosphorus views is a pleasant place to have a coffee. The best food to be had in this area is at **Kanaat**, a no-frills family-run restaurant off the main square in bustling **Üsküdar** that has been serving up traditional Turkish food since 1933.

The **hamam**, or Turkish steam bath, is an essential Istanbul experience, charmingly captured in the 1997 film *Hamam*, by Turkish-born Italian director Ferzan Ozpetek. It tells the transformative tale of an uptight Italian yuppie who inherits a derelict bathhouse in Istanbul from a long-lost aunt and eventually decides to restore it instead of selling it.

The domed marble structures are stunning feats of architecture that served an important role as communal gathering places. Modern plumbing has made the baths less necessary but there are still a few establishments that deliver the goods.

Bathers strip down to their underwear and are given a thin towel and slippers to change into. The main room is like an airy sauna, with a very high ceiling and marbled floors. You warm up by laying on a heated central slab, gazing up at the light that filters down through circular openings in the domed roof. Masseurs then scrub you down vigorously, followed by soaping and a shampoo. Squeaky clean, you round off the experience in a cooling room, with a glass of Turkish tea or freshly squeezed orange juice. Hamams typically have separate men and women's quarters. The best are **Cağaloğlu**, **Çemberlitaş** and **Galatasaray**.

‹ **Bosphorous Strait** photo: ©Steven Allan
[next page] **Hagia Sophia** photo: ©Svetlana Tikhonova

Fatih Akın, the acclaimed German-Turkish director who blasted his way onto the world stage in 2004 with *Head-On*, a turbulent love story that jumps between the two countries, lauds **Asmalımescit**, Istanbul's answer to Soho.

Once the province of embassies, Asmalımescit faded in the 1930s, when artists, bohemians and migrants from the east took up residence. Today its fortunes are on the rise again. It has become Istanbul's trendiest address, with an array of clubs (Babylon is especially popular), restaurants (Sofyalı for cheap and cheerful seafood, Otto—a pizza joint-cum-club favored by young hipsters— and the House Cafe, Istanbul's own Continental-flavored contemporary bistro chain) and hotels to match.

Gearing up for its role as European Cultural Capital 2010, Istanbul is polishing its cultural chops to become a higher profile global arts player. Plans are afoot to introduce initiatives like tax breaks and subsidies that would make filming in Turkey easier. Turkish cinema is also on the ascendant, with acclaimed directors like Nuri Bilge Ceylan, Zeki Demirkubuz and Reha Erdem part of a new generation of filmmakers that has come of age. Together, these changes could result in an increasingly diverse range of films shooting here, capturing more of the many different layers that comprise this fascinating 1,500-year-old metropolis and its 15 million inhabitants. §

Pelin Turgut writes about Turkey for a variety of publications including *Time* magazine and *The Independent*. She is also cofounder of the !f Istanbul International Independent Film Festival, held each year in February, which hosts some 70,000 people and celebrates new directions in world cinema.

06

FROM *ATONEMENT* TO *TRAINSPOTTING*
UNITED KINGDOM

TOM BEER
Most memorable film/travel experience: a showing of the Bollywood classic, *Sholay*, in New Delhi. As the audience talked, smoked, and snacked through the film, we were all transfixed by the musical melodrama of crime, revenge and redemption, responding (vocally) to everything that happened onscreen. It's the most communal moviegoing experience I've ever had.

British cinema may not have the international prestige or glamour of its continental cousins in France and Italy, but over the years, English and foreign filmmakers alike have looked from the thriving streets of London to the bucolic English countryside for British film locations. Here are some favorite movies filmed in the British Isles, and a guide to the locations where they were shot.

IN THE BEGINNING...

The county of Kent and the historic town of **Canterbury** are paid lovely tribute in Michael Powell and Emeric Pressburger's 1944 film, *A Canterbury Tale*. Powell himself was born here and spent his childhood playing amid the chestnut and hazelwood trees, the brooks and springs, and the hop fields; his affection for the landscape suffuses this strange, luminous film.

Taking inspiration from Chaucer's 14th-century classic, *A Canterbury Tale* follows three modern pilgrims: an American G.I. (Sgt. John Sweet), a British officer (Dennis Price), and an English "land girl" (Sheila Sim), one of the many women recruited for men's agricultural jobs during World War II. Stopping overnight in a small village en route to Canterbury, they encounter the "Glue Man"—an anonymous prankster who has been pouring glue in girls' hair under cover of night—and determine to solve this bizarre mystery. Yet the film reveals unexpected spiritual depths, too: each of our pilgrims has his own losses and longings; each journeys to Canterbury with hope of blessings.

The film was shot partly on location in **Kent**, and Erwin Hillier's black-and-white cinematography captures the quiet beauty of the country hills and valleys, as in the scene where Alison and Bob canter along the **Old Pilgrims' Road** in a horse and trap. The film's final sequences, which include a military parade and exterior shots of the cathedral, were filmed in Canterbury, but the Archbishop would not permit the crew inside the cathedral (a set was constructed at Denham Studios in Buckinghamshire). Happily, contemporary tourists are free to explore the historic Norman church, with its brilliant stained glass windows and vaulted ceilings. Fans can join an annual walk, led by local historian Paul Tritton, which stops at film locations.

⟨ **Canterbury Cathedral** photo: ©imbowen0306
[previous page] **Cottage in Stokesay** photo: ©ndrwfgg

SCOTLAND

Following Powell and Pressburger north to Scotland, one can tour the bleakly beautiful **Hebrides Islands** of western Scotland. Here, the traveler is reminded that Great Britain is an ancient, often mystical land, once home to the Celts. This overpowering feeling of the past is captured in *I Know Where I'm Going!*, Powell and Pressburger's extraordinary 1945 film, shot partly on the **Isle of Mull**.

The story concerns a spirited young English woman (Wendy Hiller) traveling to the fictional island of Kiloran to marry her fiancé, a wealthy

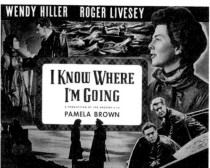

industrialist many years her senior. A sudden gale, however, prevents her from catching the ferry, and while waiting three days for the weather to clear, she falls unexpectedly in love with an appealing Scotch naval officer (Roger Livesey), descendant of one of the old local clans. *I Know Where I'm Going!* evokes a profound sense of place, and Joan's romance with Torquil is also a romance with the charm and rugged splendor of these windswept islands.

A number of Mull landmarks figure in the film, including **Torosay** and **Duart Castles**, and the picturesque fishing village of **Tobermory**. The **Western Isles Hotel**, the old Victorian guesthouse where Joan bunks down, is still in business, offering striking views of Tobermory Bay and the Sound of Mull.

Younger film viewers will likely hear Scotland and think not of medieval castles, but rather of disaffected slackers clubbing to the now ubiquitous drone of techno group Underworld. Based on a novel by Irvine Welsh, Danny Boyle's ***Trainspotting*** (1996) shone a light on the seedier side of Edinburgh—no kilts or bagpipes here (though the brogues are as thick as ever). The film chronicles the highs and lows of a group of young Scottish junkies, including Renton (Ewan McGregor), Sick Boy (Jonny Lee Miller) and Begbie (Robert Carlyle). Spiked with dark humor and a propulsive soundtrack, it was an international hit, dispatching film buffs to Edinburgh

---

^ *I Know Where I'm Going,* 1945. photo: ©Universal Pictures/Everett Collection
< [top] **Isle of Mull** photo: ©Julius Design [bottom] **Torosay Castle** photo: ©William Marnoch
[next page] **Glasgow** photo: ©Douglas McGilviray

in search of *Trainspotting* locations. Just one catch: the movie was actually made 50 miles to the west, in **Glasgow**.

Many interiors were filmed in an abandoned cigarette factory in the East End, which has since been converted into an office building. Likewise **Volcano**, the disco where Renton hooks up with underage schoolgirl Diane (Kelly McDonald), is no longer standing. But the neighborhood pub frequented by Renton's crew—and where Begbie sets off a brawl by tossing his glass over the balcony—is still here, and open for business. Go for a pint and rub shoulders with ordinary Glaswegians at **Crosslands** on Queen Margaret Drive.

THE GRAND ESTATES

If you're looking for an English country house for a film location, what better place than the pages of *Country Life* magazine, dedicated to England's "premium" properties? That's where production designer Sarah Greenwood found an article on **Stokesay Court**, a grand Victorian manor that stands in for Tallis House in *Atonement* (2007), director Joe Wright's Oscar-winning adaptation of the novel by Ian McEwan.

Atonement is the story of an upper-class family, the Tallises, and what unfolds on one summer day in 1935 when naïve young Briony Tallis (Saoirse Rowan) walks in on her sister Cecilia (Keira Knightley) *in flagrante delicto* with the housekeeper's son, Robbie (James McAvoy)—and mistakenly believes that he is attacking her. This misunderstanding, and Briony's subsequent accusation, will have tragic consequences for all three characters.

The scenes at Tallis House evoke the luxurious life enjoyed by the English upper classes during the years between World War I and World War II, when people dressed for dinner and were waited on by a regiment of servants. Naturally, Stokesay Court—near the village of **Onibury, Shropshire**, in the

West Midlands—is the genuine article. Built in 1891 by a wealthy glove merchant on more than 100 acres of land, the house is today is privately owned but open for public tours.

And if we continue to tour the grand estates of Britain, two generations of film viewers will recognize **Castle Howard in Yorkshire** as Brideshead, the stately country seat of the Marchmain family in adaptations of Evelyn Waugh's classic novel, *Brideshead Revisited*. First used for location shooting in the 1981 television miniseries starring Jeremy Irons, the castle again doubled for Brideshead in last summer's big-screen version by director Julian Jarrold.

Brideshead Revisited tells the story of Charles Ryder (played by Matthew Goode in the 2008 film), a middle-class student at Oxford who befriends charismatic Sebastian Flyte (Ben Whishaw) and is taken into the bosom of Sebastian's aristocratic, Anglo-Catholic family, the Marchmains. Charles, an aesthete and later an architectural painter, is as much seduced by Brideshead castle as he is by the family that lives in it, and is thrilled when Lady Marchmain (Emma Thompson) asks him to paint a series of murals in one of the rooms.

HITCHCOCK'S LONDON

The great Alfred Hitchcock, whose film career was split between England and Hollywood, took delight in staging scenes at iconic landmarks: think of Mount Rushmore (*North by Northwest*), the Golden Gate Bridge (*Vertigo*), and the Statue of Liberty (*Saboteur*). But Hitchcock was a Londoner born and bred, and some of his greatest sequences take place in the English capital.

A few highlights:

In **Blackmail** (1929), England's first talkie, the blackmailer (Donald Calthorp), is pursued by police into the British Museum and through the Egyptian galleries, meeting his end on the dome atop the immense Round Reading Room.

In **Sabotage** (1936), a terrorist (Oskar Homolka) plunges London into a blackout when he commits an act of sabotage at a power plant—in fact the Battersea Power Station (familiar to later generations from the cover of Pink Floyd's *Animals*).

In both versions of **The Man Who Knew Too Much** (1934 and 1956) Hitchcock set a climactic set piece in London's famous Royal Albert Hall. The story concerns a couple whose child has been kidnapped by a sinister group planning to assassinate a foreign prime minister. The assassination attempt takes place during an orchestral concert at the Hall—but is thwarted by the mother's blood-curdling scream.

After 20 years in Hollywood, Hitchcock returned to London to make his penultimate film, **Frenzy** (1972). It's

a dark tale about a serial killer who rapes women and strangles them with a necktie. A down-on-his-luck barman (Jon Finch) is framed for the crimes, while the real killer stalks his ex-wife (Barbara Leigh-Hunt) and current girlfriend (Anna Massey).

From its opening credit sequence—shot from a helicopter swooping along the Thames River and appearing to pass under the raised bascules of Tower Bridge—*Frenzy* is a tribute to the city Hitchcock knew and loved. Many of the exteriors were shot in Covent Garden, then the city's fruit, vegetable and flower market. Only two years later the market was moved to Nine Elms, and so the scenes in *Frenzy* are a final document of the old Covent Garden—today a gentrified neighborhood of boutiques and fancy shops.

The British Museum
Great Russell Street, London
www.britishmuseum.org
+44 (0)20 7323 8299

Royal Albert Hall
Kensington Gore, London
www.royalalberthall.com
020 7838 3105 (to book a tour)

Tower Bridge
www.towerbridge.org.uk
020 7940 3984 (call to find out when the bridge is being raised)

Covent Garden
Take the Tube to Covent Garden station
Long Acre and James streets

Castle Howard has a pedigree every bit as exalted as its fictional counterpart. In 1699 the Earl of Carlisle commissioned Sir John Vanbrugh—a novice architect—to build him the house; Vanbrugh, along with Nicholas Hawksmoor, was responsible for the design of the main house. The castle is indeed distinctive, with its magnificent Great Hall and the dome above, the Atlas fountain, the Temple of the Four Winds—plus one thousand acres of lawns, gardens, lakes, and woodlands. Castle Howard and its grounds are open to members of the public, who like Charles Ryder, can fall in love with its grand follies.

THE BEACHES

Few film locations in Great Britain have been used to better effect than **Holy Island**, the eerie setting for Roman Polanski's *Cul-de-Sac* (1966). Situated in far northeast England, Holy Island is connected to the mainland of Northumberland by only a narrow causeway, and when the tide is high the island is inaccessible except by boat. In ancient times, it was the site of a monastery where St. Cuthbert resided briefly, and the monks here produced the illuminated Lindisfarne Gospels.

In *Cul-de-Sac*, **Lindisfarne Castle**—perched upon an imposing rock outcropping—is home to a

> **Holy Island, Lindisfarne** photo: ©JayKay57

quarrelsome couple (Donald Pleasance and Françoise Dorléac), held hostage by a buffoonish gangster (Lionel Stander), who appears to be fleeing a botched deal and is awaiting rescue by his boss, the mysterious Mr. Katelbach. We're in Samuel Beckett territory here, and the stark island is a perfect, otherworldly backdrop to this comic existential drama.

Now picture the English seaside, with its gaudy attractions and questionable weather, and you're likely to conjure up **Brighton**, the southeastern coastal town that is synonymous with holiday weekending. A quick jaunt from London by train, Brighton was put on the map by the Prince of the Wales (later George IV) who entertained his mistress here in the late 18th century.

So iconic is Brighton that more than 50 films have been shot here, including The Who's cult classic, *Quadrophenia* (1979). But perhaps the greatest film set in and about the seaside community is John Boulting's *Brighton Rock* (1947), which cements the association of Brighton with a low-life element. It's a tense film noir based on the novel by Graham Greene. Richard Attenborough stars as Pinky, a baby-faced hoodlum who runs a criminal racket in Brighton and marries a naïve young waitress (Carol Marsh) to keep her from testifying against him in a murder case. (The film's title, incidentally, refers to a kind of candy cane typically sold at resorts and is used in the film to choke a character to death.)

Footage of typical Brighton scenes—the beach, the **Royal Pavilion**, the **racetrack**—was shot on location. So was part of the climactic confrontation with Pinky on the Palace Pier (now called the **Brighton Pier**), a famous symbol of Brighton with its brightly illuminated arcades, restaurants, and theaters.

LONDON

Director Woody Allen is one of the great chroniclers of New York in the movies, but for his 2005 picture, *Match Point*, he crossed the pond to shoot in **London**, and critics felt that the new location gave his work a new fizz. Allen is

^ *Quadrophenia*, 1978. photo: ©Rex Features/Everett Collection
‹ [top] **Brighton Beach, UK** photo: ©johnny boy A
[bottom] **Entrance, Tate Modern** photo: ©Matthias Wasserman

definitely an outsider in the city—he doesn't seem to capture its essence the way he does New York's—but he's a tourist having a fabulous time, and it shows.

Match Point is about a calculating and ambitious tennis pro (Jonathan Rhys Meyers) who gains the trust of a wealthy family, becomes engaged to the

daughter (Emily Mortimer) and begins a disastrous affair with his brother-in-law's sultry fiancée (Scarlett Johansson). For one crucial scene, Allen deposits his characters in the **Tate Modern**, a museum housed in the vast industrial space of the Bankside Power Station. The place is truly enormous (it's billed as the largest modern art museum in the word) and allows Allen's characters to give one another the slip and secretly rendezvous amidst the Rothkos, Warhols, and Hirsts.

Antonioni's *Blow-Up* (1966) heralded the advent of the 1960s' Swinging London, a swirling center of fashion, art, music and drugs. Antonioni's protagonist is Thomas, a cocky young photographer (David Hemmings) who wanders into a London park and surreptitiously photographs an enigmatic woman (Vanessa Redgrave) having a liaison with an older man. Later, developing and enlarging his pictures, he realizes he has photographed a dead body in the background.

The park at the center of *Blow-Up*'s mystery is **Maryon Park** in Charlton, a leafy little enclave in Southeast London. The antiques shop where Thomas buys an airplane propeller is no longer there (it was a grocery, in reality), but you can still see the White Horse Pub (704 Woolwich Rd.), where the cast and crew waited out a rainstorm during the shoot. A stroll through the park reveals the courts where *Blow-Up*'s troupe of white-faced mimes played a ball-less game of tennis. Just don't be surprised if the grass isn't as strikingly green as in the film; Antonioni literally had it painted to achieve the visual effect he wanted. §

Tom Beer has written about film for *Time Out New York* and *Newsday*. His travel stories have appeared in *Culture + Travel, 360*, and on Frommers.com.

^ *Match Point,* 2005. photo: ©DreamWorks/Everett Collection
‹ **English pub** photo: ©Flaviana Bottazzini

07

DARK SPACE/ WHITE SPACE

SCANDINAVIA

ENRIQUE RAMIREZ
Most memorable film/travel experience: Getting a chance in 2007 to visit Hans Scharoun's Berlin Stadtbibliothek, the library depicted in Wim Wenders' *Wings of Desire*— it was magical.

Scandinavia is a region of extremes, and
this is not a bad thing. In fact, it is precisely this oscillation
between extremes—stylish metropoles and barren countryside,
placid gardens and active volcanoes, Norwegian Black Metal
and Aqua—that makes Scandinavia such a fascinating region of
the world. One could even attribute this presence of extremes
to the region's unique climate. Ask a resident of Copenhagen
about the seasons in Denmark, and he or she is likely to say
something glib like, "There's summer, and winter. And winter.
And winter. And winter."

Climate is the sun's relationship to the world, and light is manipulated to
create moods and atmospheres that create the moving images that flicker
across the movie screen. It is possible then to start considering Scandinavian
cinema in terms of how light is captured and manipulated. In order to do
this, a brief tour of Scandinavia's most famous studios is in order.

FILM CITIES IN DENMARK

A smallish municipality about 13 kilometers southwest of Copenhagen,
Denmark, Hvidovre is a place steeped in rich history. A Bronze Age sword
was found there in 1929. It was also the site of a major battle between Danish
resistance fighters and members of the Nazi-backed HIPO auxiliary police.

Today, this site is known as **Filmbyen**, or "Film City" (which is open to the
public). Here, nestled among the various offices and sound stages, one finds
the offices for Zentropa Film, is Lars von Trier's production company. Named
after von Trier's critically acclaimed 1991 film of the same name, today
Zentropa is the largest film production company in Scandinavia. Its output
is impressive. This studio is the site of at least 70 major theatrical releases,
four of which have gone on to receive Best Foreign Film nominations at the
Academy Awards, others have received Palmes d'Or at Cannes and Silver
Bears at the Berlin Film Festival.

Film City is a unique place. In 2003, the *Guardian*'s Damon Wise spent
the day with von Trier and observed the various rituals that take place in this
most unusual of settings. Newly-minted scripts are ceremoniously dunked in
a cup of tea that used to belong to auteur Carl Theodore Dreyer (1889-1968),

---

‹ **Filmbyen** photo: ©Dan Phiffer
[previous page] **Oslo in winter** photo: ©Tyler Olson

who single-handedly placed Denmark on the cinema with films like *The Passion of Joan of Arc* (1928), *Vampyr* (1932) and *Day of Wrath* (1943). Flags are raised and pipes are played whenever a new production commences. One wonders if such displays are truly the sign of a remarkable movement or an all-too-visible provincialism.

Most likely, it is the former. Although Zentropa will forever be associated with von Trier, considered one of Denmark's most important directors, it is also the birthplace of the Dogme 95 movement. A film that exemplifies the Dogme spirit best is *The Celebration* (1998). Here, director Thomas Vinterberg uses handheld video cameras to capture all types of light—

natural and artificial—to give the film a distinct, near-documentary feel. It is as if Vinterberg were actually participating in the events that drive the storyline along. The film was shot in **Skjoldenæsholm**, a stately manor in Jystup, about 60 km west of Copenhagen. This palatial, neoclassical 18th century residence (now serving as a hotel and conference center) exemplifies a type of architectural restraint that echoes Dogme's cinematic pragmatism, for though it does not have an ornate façade, its sheer size—and a lavish interior filled with the impeccable designs of early Danish furniture—more than compensate.

One of Skjoldenæsholm manor's most distinguishing features is **Valsølille**, a lake that borders the rear of the house. During the height of midsummer, the lake captures the white late-evening sun, casting it against the manor's flat granite walls. These natural settings are also featured in an earlier film, Poul Bang's *I Kongens Klæ'r* (1954), a crime caper about mistaken identities. But in *The Celebration*, the effect of the light bouncing from Valsølille is anything but comic. The titular birthday celebration is continuously bathed in light, either sunlight reflecting off Valsølille, or candlelight. It is ironic how this undiluted Nordic light does as much to expose the characters' own dark, inner urgings and sordid pasts.

⌃ *The Celebration*, 1998. photo: ©October Films/Everett Collection
‹ **Skjoldenæsholm Train** photo: ©thy
[next page] **Copenhagen** photo: ©JC i Nuria

TROLLS AND GARBO IN SWEDEN

Situated in the evergreen ravines and running snowmelt of the **Göta River** in Västra Götaland, Sweden, is the mid-sized city of **Trollhättan**. Continuously

inhabited for 7,000 years, Trollhättan is an important location in the Swedish imagination. Trollhättan is also the home of **Film i Väst**, one of Scandinavia's largest film production facilities. Like Filmbyen, this facility was founded in the 1990s as part of a regional development fund. Headed by Tomas Eskilsson and Bengt Toll, Film i Väst has been responsible for over 200 films. The very first film made there was Lukas Moodysson's controversial *Fucking Åmål* (1998, American title: *Show Me Love*). Today, the studio continues to host some high-profile productions. Even Lars von Trier produced two of his most well-known recent pictures at Film i Väst: *Dancer in the Dark* (2000) and *Dogville* (2003).

If an enterprising tourist interested in Scandinavian cinema were to cross the Baltic to Stockholm and land at Frihamnen, he or she would catch a bus at Frihamnenporten station. From there, the bus would travel along Lindarängsvägen and end up on Borgvägen street. Getting off the bus, a long, brutalist concrete building will confront their gaze. This building, designed by the prolific modernist Peter Celsing in 1970, is home to the **Swedish Film Institute** (Svenska Filminstitutet, open to the public). Celsing's concrete temple to film is an obsessively orthogonal 140-meter long slab. Its crenellated roof reminds one of a fortification or a bulwark, but if anything, it stands as a direct contrast to the Tessinparken's green expanse. Although the Filmhuset is a working facility, showing just how much film is the lifeblood of Sweden's cultural life, there is plenty there for the cinephile to enjoy. For example, the building houses the Swedish Film Library, home to over 50,000 books and film-related materials, and the Bildarkivets, a collection of stills and posters from Swedish cinema. During summers, the Institute hosts a Cinemathqeue series, screening retrospectives as well as archival material. The Filmbuteken, a store on the ground level, offers a wide variety of film titles for sale (and its online version offers many of these as digital downloads). And last but not least, there is a bar and a restaurant.

⌃ **Lars von Trier,** 2000. photo: ©Miramax Films/Everett Collection
⌄ **Goeta River** photo: ©Johan Larsson

Moving from east to west across Scandinavia, one could find various places, all depicted in film, that capitalize on capturing sunlight's horizontal transit. The most famous is Erik Skjoldbjærg's *Insomnia* (1997), parts of which were filmed in Norway's northernmost reaches, in **Tromsø**. This city of 64,000 is situated about 220 miles (350 km) north of the Arctic Circle. Incidentally, it is also home to the oldest existing theatre in Scandinavia, the **Verdensteatret Kinematograpf**, originally built in 1916.

LETTERS FROM ICELAND

Iceland is an even more remote example of the Nordic landscape. This piece of highly volcanic real estate in the North Atlantic Ocean, features some stark lunar landscapes that, when filmed in the height of winter, provide a desired. One of the most famous recent examples is Friðrik Þór Friðriksson's 1995 film, *Á köldum klaka* (*Cold Fever*). Here, a young Japanese businessman named Hirata (Masatoshi Nagase) travels to Iceland to perform the last rites for his parents, who died in a river while touring there years ago. Light and landscape literally fill up the frame. A flat, white expanse of snowdrifts is interrupted by ashen crags of ice and rock. A frozen waterfall turns blue in the frozen air. In one scene, Hirata bathes in a hot spring. The calm water reflects the evening sky to great effect: it is as if earth and sky were meeting in Iceland.

Although *Cold Fever* offers a panoramic tour of many of Iceland's visual offerings, some of these sights have recurring roles in other films. Yet these films do not take place in Iceland. It is as if this small country's rich visual offerings stand for something more universal. Take, for example, Clint Eastwood's 2006 war epic *Flags of Our Fathers*. Though the film is supposed to depict the harrowing invasion and battle for Iwo Jima in the South Pacific, the film was actually shot in **Sandvik**, a beach on the southwestern coast of Iceland. The film's location scouts and managers were pointed to Iceland by a gas station attendant, who when asked if he knew of any black sand beaches with volcanoes, replied, "You mean like the ones in Iceland?"

Iceland is not the only remote Nordic outpost that has been committed to celluloid. Parts of Bille August's adaptation of Peter Høeg's *Smilla's Sense of Snow* were filmed in **Ilulissat**, a glacier town that is Greenland's most popular tourist destination. Faroese director Katrin Ottarsdóttir has been shooting all her films in **Tórshavn**, the capital of the Faroe Islands. Her most famous feature, *Atlantic Rhapsody - 52 myndir úr Tórshavn* (1990) is a perfect introduction to this remote Danish principality: it depicts 52 real-time minutes in Tórshavn.

NORDIC METROPOLES

There are also some notable examples where the Nordic metropolis is depicted in such a way as to capitalize on its ability to capture light. Petter Næss's *Elling* (2001) was shot almost entirely in the **Majorstuen** section of Oslo. In one scene, the titular character (Per Christian Ellefsen) and his sidekick, Kjell Bjarne (Sven Nordlin) travel with a social worker from Majorstuen station along some of Oslo's major streets. Through the windows of a taxicab, we get to know this city at the same time as the characters. It is a bustling place filled with light and commotion. Part of this is from the signage, of course. But once we see Elling and Kjell Bjarne in their apartment, we again see the filtered white light that is so characteristic of this part of the world.

Copenhagen has also been the setting for classic cinematic fare. For example, the luxurious **Hotel d'Angleterre** in the Kongens Nytorv section of Copenhagen is the setting for Alfred Hitchcock's *Torn Curtain* (1966) and

Topaz (1969). *Torn Curtain* not only begins with an establishing shot of the **Tivoli Gardens**, but the film's two main characters, played by Paul Newman and Julie Andrews, even eat inside the Tivoli's glassed-in *Nimb* restaurant. In addition to a few scenes shot alongside the **Nyhavn Canal**, one famous scene inside the Hotel d'Angleterre features an Alfred Hitchcock cameo. *Topaz*, on the other hands, offers more standard Copenhagen fare. The film's main character, CIA agent Michael Nordstrom, is seen beside some of Copenhagen's more famous landmarks, including the Rådhuspladsen (City Hall Square), the Royal Copenhagen Porcelain factory, and the Vesterport station (on Vesterbrogade).

⌃ **Tivoli Gardens** photo: ©gary718
⌲ **Majorstuen, Oslo** photo: ©Tomoyoshi

Helsinki's proximity to Eastern Europe and the former Soviet Union made it an ideal location to shoot scenes that were supposed to take place in Moscow or St. Petersburg. Helsinki's **Senate Square**, bordered on one side by the Office of the Prime Minister and by the University of Helsinki on the other, was dressed to look like Leningrad in Warren Beatty's *Reds* (1981). More recently, the last segment of Jim Jarmusch's likable taxicab romp *Night on Earth* (1991) was shot along Senate Square. The fact that this is a location of high cinematic import is emphasized by the fact the driver of Jarmusch's Helsinki taxi is none other than Matti Pellonpää, one of Finland's most famous actors to date.

Of course no discussion of sublime depictions of city, landscape, and light in Scandinavia can continue without considering Ingmar Bergman. Although many of Bergman's most famous films were shot at Svenska Filmindustri's Filmstaden facility, his depiction of **Lake Vättern** in *Wild Stawberries* deserves special mention. Located in south-central Sweden, Vättern is Europe's fifth-largest lake. Known for its crystalline waters, it is also a popular vacation spot. During the winter, Swedes go to the various spas in surrounding towns like Vadstena, Jönköping, Hjo, Askersund, Åmmeberg, and Karlsborg. During the summer, Vättern's banks and nearby glades are covered with grass, elderberry, as well as the wild strawberry patches from Bergman's film. Isak Borg's time travel from Stockholm to Lund takes a serious and meaningful detour once he arrives on the shores of Lake Vättern. In a series of memory-induced hallucinations, Borg goes beyond recalling events from his youth—he witnesses moments that he did not participate in.

In many ways, Vättern is the quintessentially Nordic film location. Not only does it figure prominently in what is perhaps one of the best-loved Swedish films, but stands for many of the things pointed out in this piece. It is a place that captures the region's seasonal fluctuations between darkness and light. Vättern is also one of Scandinavia's signature landmarks, a place that is as familiar as Norway's fjords, Iceland's volcanoes and glaciers, or even Copenhagen's Tivoli and Rådhuspladsen. It is a must-see for the cineaste that just happens to be taking a tour of this part of the world. §

Enrique Ramirez is an architecture historian who writes about cities and film, and fortunately has time to travel.

< [top] **Senate Square, Helsinki** photo: ©jimg944
[bottom] **Lake Vättern** photo: ©Marcus Lindstrom

08

FROM RUSSIA,
WITH LUXE

RUSSIA

LAUREL MAURY
Most memorable film/travel experience: Walking through
Pavlosk Park in the twilight of the white nights. The place
has an eerie beauty, like the gardens of Versailles mixed
with '70s housing and a run-down carnival.

In Sergei Eisenstein's beloved *Alexander Nevsky* (1938), the hero says to the Mongol leader, "Better to die in your own land than leave it." Yet despite Russians' deep love for the motherland, many of the great Soviet films were not, in fact, shot at home. *Battleship Potemkin* (1925), *Ivan the Terrible* (1944)—except for a few scenes possibly shot in Nizhni Novgorod—*The Diamond Arm* (1968), perhaps the Soviet Union's most popular comedy, and many others were shot in outlying Soviet Republics.

During World War II, the fledgling Communist country's best filmmakers were evacuated to **Baku**, in Azerbaijan, or to **Almaty**, in Kazakhstan, where they continued to make "Russian" classics for years. Shooting in the Soviet Republics was dirt cheap, and had the potential benefit of spreading patriotism to regions unhappy at being forced into the Soviet fold. Plus, the Russian winter is hard on equipment; **St. Petersburg** in particular isn't exactly conducive to winter filmmaking. This, Russia's most beautiful city, is called the Venice of the north, yet it is plunged into darkness three months of the year and its canals are frozen for nearly four months, making it less the second Serenissima and more the dark inside of the refrigerator.

So when Tarkovsky's young Ivan runs along the banks of a river in *My Name is Ivan* (1962), he's actually running in Kanev, on the Ukrainian rather than the Russian part of the Dneiper. Eisenstein's Ivan in *Ivan the Terrible* goes slowly mad not in **Moscow's Kremlin**, but in a soundstage probably located in Baku. When the baby bounces down the steps in *Battleship Potemkin*, it does so in Odessa. And in Josef Heifitz's masterpiece *The Woman with the Small Dog* (1960), based on Anton Chekhov's short story of the same title, Gurov seduces Anna Sergeevna in **Yalta**—part of the Russian Crimea then, the Ukraine, now.

Finally, in many instances Russian directors were far more concerned with the internal landscapes of their films, and the emotions they could evoke in viewers, than external imagery. Many films were made to inspire workers and thus concerned the "everyman" or "everywoman" and presented stories not tied to any specific locale. Eisenstein's *Old and New* (1929), a film about the trials and successes of a collective farm, for example, was shot in and around Rostov-on-Don but was meant to represent scenes taking place all over Russia, so there's little about the film that's location-specific. (Eisenstein didn't feel it needed to be actor-specific either, so when good Stanislavski-trained actresses turned up their noses at milking cows and plowing, he cast an illiterate peasant woman, Marfa Lapkina, as the lead.) Unless a scene was tied to the Revolution, specific settings simply weren't a priority in Soviet film. And with all the footage and notes destroyed by censors and German bombs, discovering where many of these films were shot can be quite difficult.

FLYING INTO RUSSIA

As you fly into either St. Petersburg or Moscow, endless vast fields of Soviet-era apartment blocks surround each city like the dull, gray ring on a bathtub. Jokes about the sameness of these apartment blocks abound in Soviet film, and it's the very subject of Emil Braginsky's *Irony of Fate* (1971). Braginsky's hero, Luzhen, passes out drunk in Moscow on New Year's Eve. As a joke, his friends put him on a plane to St. Petersburg. Luzhen wakes up, goes to the same apartment in the same building, on the same block—not noticing he's in a different city. His key fits in the door, and he clambers, half-asleep, into bed, only to wake up with the wrong woman! *Irony of Fate* is shown every New Year's Eve in Russia, much as *It's a Wonderful Life* is shown in America on Christmas. Part of the irony is that no one seems to know which apartment buildings were actually used for the film shoot.

ST. PETERSBURG

One place where film lovers can still find specific locations is in St. Petersburg. The city has gone through three names in less than a century, but its late 18th- and early 19th-century city center, a study in muted pastels, has remained largely unchanged.

The **Hermitage Museum** is a vast, baroque confection, yet warm and light. It was once the tsar's Winter Palace and is the setting for Alexsander Sukurov's *Russian Ark* (2002). Made in one long tracking shot that moves through 33

‹ **St. Petersburg** photo: ©Akira Chiba

rooms of the 18th-century building, Sukurov's time-traveling vision shifts from the decades of Catherine the Great to the era of Pushkin to the present and back.

The **Hermitage Theater**, where Russian Ark's unnamed, ghostly narrator happens upon the backstage activity of an 18th-century opera, was designed by Giacomo Quarenghi, who brought Palladian architecture to Russia in force. This theater regularly shows some of the greatest opera in the world—productions that Westerners rarely see.

In *Russian Ark*, the narrator and his companion, the Marquis de Custine, come upon Tsar Nicholas I and his court receiving emissaries from the Shah of Iran in the St. George Hall. The movie culminates in a grand 19th-century ball shot in the Armorial Hall, where the tsars once held their grand receptions. No less than Valery Gergiev, Russia's greatest living conductor, leads the orchestra. The movie exits out the grand Council Staircase.

This staircase may also be seen in *Ten Days that Shook The World*, Eisenstein's 1927 reenactment of the October Revolution of 1917, in which a constipated-looking Alexander Karensky and his entourage mince daintily up the marble stairs in shiny boots to see the tsar. Eisenstein cuts footage of Karensky with footage of the tsar's mechanical Peacock Clock, a famous early use of montage created to suggest that Russia's prime minister was as empty-headed as the bird. The clock itself, which still works, can be found in the Hermitage's Pavilion Hall. Another famous shot of Karensky shows him in the rooms of Tsar Alexander III, intimating that he's spoiling to become Alexander IV. It's actually Nicholas II's wood-paneled library. When Eisenstein shot this film, the Russian Revolution was only ten years old, and many of the rooms in the Winter Palace, most likely including this one, were still more or less as they had been when Lenin screamed his head off at Finland Station. Certainly, it's full of the bizarre Victorian bric-a-brac Russia's last tsar loved.

^ *Russian Ark,* 2002. photo: ©Wellspring/Everett Collection
< **Mariinsky Theater, St. Petersburg** photo: ©Sergey I

Russian Ark also shows tantalizing glimpses of the Hermitage's "back rooms." Actually, the museum has a storage facility in **Staraya Derevnaya**, outside the city center. There, visitors may see four royal coronation carriages, including that of Nicholas II. Also present is the furniture of the Romanovs and an enormous fancy tent. Given to Catherine the Great, it's a Barnum & Bailey-sized contraption of embroidered yellow silk. Apparently no one knew what to do with it, as it's been kept in storage for 200 years.

The Winter Palace is stormed in *Ten Days that Shook the World*. It's a standing joke that more people were hurt in Eisenstein's shoot in the **Palace Square** than in the relatively bloodless October coup—either due to organizational sloppiness or a deep commitment to naturalistic acting, some of the bullets Eisenstein used were real. But when, to make the Winter Palace chandeliers shake, suggesting a gun barrage, Eisenstein ordered the cannons of the battleship **Aurora** fired, no one was hurt. The Aurora, now a museum ship in St. Petersburg Harbor, is open every Wednesday through Friday.

A stunning walk that will let you take in the city's famous drawbridges starts at the corner of **Sadovaya Street** (Sadovaya Ulitsa) and **Nevsky Prospect** (Nevsky Prospekt). This is a corner where Eisenstein shot many of his crowd scenes, cranking the camera at different speeds to visually suggest differing levels of panic. Turn northeast along Nevsky. The Soviet administrative offices have been replaced with swank shops, but the 19th-century architecture is intact. Take a quick right on Admiralty Prospect, and then left onto Dvortsovyy Drive (Dvortsovyy Proyezd). To the right will be the Winter Palace. Straight on leads to Admiralty Embankment (Admiraltiskaya Naberezhnaya), along the Nevsky River.

The drawbridges opening along the Neva are an unearthly sight. Every night between 2 and 5 AM the lovely arched bridges go up, and Russian submarines and ships pass underneath. Lovers stay to watch during the White Nights in early summer. If you're out late, make sure you're on the correct side of the river before 2 AM hits.

If you want to eat while you watch the boats, try the **White Lady Cat/ Black Tomcat Café** (Beliya Koshka/Chyornij Kot, 13/15 Pestelya Street), which serves reasonably priced Serbian cuisine. Later in the evening, the

---

> [top] **The Church of Our Savior on Spilled Blood, St. Petersburg** photo: ©Akira Chiba
> [bottom] **Dvortsovy Bridge, St. Petersburg** photo: ©Akira Chiba

café takes up the tables and turns into a bar and disco. This friendly eatery is next to the **Smolny Cathedral**, which also played a pivotal part in the Revolution and is the location of the Bolshevik offices in *Ten Days that Shook the World*.

The nearby suburb of **Tsarskoe Selo** is the setting for *1814* (2007), a costume drama-cum-mystery that focuses on the schooldays of poet Alexander Pushkin, future statesman Prince Alexander Gorkachov, poet and journalist Anton Delvig, and the Decembrist poet Wilhelm Kuchelbecker. These future greats attended the Tsarskoe Selo Lyceum together, the abandoned buildings of which may be found on Academicheskii Street. The film was shot in and around the town without the addition of a single decoration to spruce up the interiors.

Although not a masterpiece, this clever little thriller is a good example of the thin walls that separate Russian film, Russian television and Russian theater. The film was released both in cinemas and as a televised miniseries. A quick look at the biographies of the young actors reveals that they've done as much serious theater work as anything else.

MOSCOW

Although the **Kremlin** has been Russia's center of power on and off for hundreds of years, few films have been shot there—the Soviet

government didn't want its administrative buildings on camera. However the recent pop-culture masterpiece, *Tycoon* (2002), starring Slavic heartthrob Vladimir Mashkov, has many scenes shot near and even in this famous red citadel along the River Moskva. (Mashkov, who had a supporting role in *Behind Enemy Lines* (2001), is rumored to be the inspiration for Nico Bellic in *Grand Theft Auto IV*).

Although information is scant, it appears that Eisenstein never shot a single scene of *Ivan the Terrible* here, though much of the tsar's life took

---

∧ *Tycoon,* 2002. photo: ©Arte/Everett Collection

< [top] **Statue of Pushkin** photo: ©Ekaterina Starshaya
 [bottom] **Moscow Subway** photo: ©Losevsky Pavel

place where the Soviet government later sat. Rather, the external scenes appear to have been shot in Tver. However, the real crown worn by Russia's most terrifying tsar, called **Monomakh's Cap** (Shapka Monomaxa), may be seen in the Kremlin armory. Not far away, **Lomonosov Moscow State University**, one of Stalin's seven Constructivist "Wedding Cake" buildings and the main building for one of the great universities of the world was the setting for Leonid Gadai's *Operation Y* (1965). This pastel-painted former stronghold of Soviet learning—complete with oversized clock—looks like something Disney might manufacture out of Legos for the *It's a Small World* ride. You sense that comic master Gaidai, who recognized a good joke when he saw one, knew this.

Travelers can experience the utmost in Russian gilt and glitter at **Turandot**, a lavish restaurant at 26/5 Tverskoi Bulvar. The establishment seems to channel both 1890s splendor and the extravagance of the modern oligarch. It's either a baroque monstrosity or a baroque masterpiece—no one's quite sure which—but it's the lunch spot for the wives and girlfriends of Russia's nouveau riche (the only kind of riche they've got). At the center, a trio of musicians in 18th-century attire plays beneath a gilded tree—on which sits a gigantic golden peacock based on the same Peacock Clock in the Hermitage that Eisenstein used to make Karensky look like a dandified fool. Although no films have been shot here as yet, this restaurant plays a huge role in how the new Russia sees itself. Expensive, rococo and almost a cartoon of wealth, it's rumored to be oddly empty since the financial crash. Strangely, it serves Chinese food.

For a more somber scene, try the Stalinist-era **Embankment House** built on the banks of the Moskva River. In Mikhalkov's *Burnt by the Sun* (1994), Mitia, the worrying NKVD officer come to arrest the kindly Kotov and take him away from his beloved granddaughter, lives in Embankment House. A masterpiece of Constructivism—which can be only described as Art Deco gone rectangular and a bit silly—Embankment House is famous not for being a holdout for the secret police, but rather for being a place from which an estimated one-third of the tenants, the upper-echelon of Soviet society, were made to disappear by the secret police. The building, now a sought-after residence, has an upscale grocery store and a small museum. Please ignore the massive Mercedes symbol slowly rotating on top of what should be a World Heritage site.

> **Assumption Cathedral, Kremlin** photo: ©Alexander Avdeev

Half a day's drive out of Moscow along the Gorkovskoe Highway, **Vladimir** was once a medieval capital of Russia. The icons shown at the end of Tartovsky's *The Passion of Andrei Rublev* (1960) may be found here in the **Dormition Cathedral**. Part of the Golden Ring of important religious towns outside of Moscow, Vladimir is a mix of old wooden church buildings and modern chemical factories.

YALTA AND SOCHI

Yalta, now part of the Ukraine, was where Russians once shot their beach and resort films—it was the Eastern European Malibu. Lately vacationers have shifted to **Sochi**, which offers warm pebble beaches backed by mountains with excellent skiing. (Sochi's ski resort, Krasnaya Polyana, is set to be the home of the 2014 Winter Olympics.) East of Sochi, the scenic **Mzimta River** has been the setting for many movies, including *Roman and Francheska* (1960). The Mzimta's Ah-Tsu gorge was the setting for *Kidnapping, Caucasian-Style* (1967), by Gadai. It's a great area for either hiking or rafting. Contact the Radisson SAS Lazurnaya Hotel to arrange for a guide—but do use a guide. With the nearby Ossetian conflict, who knows when the Caucasians will resurrect their fine old tradition of kidnapping. Also, the Ah-Tsu gorge is particularly treacherous; one spot is called "God, Pass by Danger."

Lastly, for a weird hotel experience, try the **Grand Hotel Rodina**, at 33 Vinogradanaya Street. This Stalinist-era villa has marble interiors, a private beachfront and a library of rare Russian books. (Rumor is they're turning the bomb shelter into a cigar bar.) For a place that's more authentic, and tacky, but less pricey and clean, the **Fidan** complex (www.fidan-sochi.ru) off Kyrotnij Prospect offers cozy rooms, local cuisine and a traditional Russian banya. If you're there in July and August, be sure to sample some pickled suluguni cheese, the tiny local strawberries and the Caucasian peaches, which can reach the size of small terriers. §

Laurel Maury has had a fascination with Russian literature her entire life. She traveled to the Soviet Union as a child and to Russia as an adult. She reviews books for *The Los Angeles Times* and graphic novels for NPR.

READING / VIEWING
APPENDIX

SUGGESTED READING/VIEWING

On Location: Cities of the World in Film, 2006.
Hellmann, Claudia & Weber-Hof, Claudine, Munich: Bucher Publishing.

The Worldwide Guide to Movie Locations, 2001.
Reeves, Tony, London: Titan Books.

*Dogme Uncut: Lars von Trier, Thomas Vinterberg,
and the Gang That Took on Hollywood*, 2003.
Stevenson, Jack, Santa Monica: Santa Monica Press.

Once Upon a Time in Italy: The Westerns of Sergio Leone, 2005.
Frayling, Christopher, London: Thames & Hudson Ltd.

BFI Film Classics: Lawrence of Arabia, 2007.
Jackson, Kevin, London: British Film Institute.

Documenting Spain, 2005.
Mendelson, Jordana, University Park: Pennsylvania State University Press.

My Last Sigh, 2003.
Buñuel, Luis, St. Paul: University of Minnesota Press.

Ghosts of Spain: Travels Through Spain and Its Silent Past, 2008.
Tremlett, Giles, New York: Walker & Company.

INDEX + CREDITS
FILM

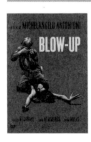

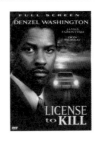

FILM	YEAR	DVD DISTRIBUTOR	CHAPTER	PAGE
Spirit of the Beehive, The	1973	Criterion	Spain	25
Star Maker	1996	Miramax Home Ent	Italy	67
Straight to Hell	1987	Starz	Spain	13
Stromboli	1950	n/a	Italy	67
Summer's Tale, A	1996	Fox Lorber	France	35
Talented Mr. Ripley, The	1999	Paramount	Italy	62
Teenage Wolfpack	1956	Interwest	Germany	71
Ten Days that Shook the World	1927	Amkino Corporation	Russia	145
This Man Must Die	1969	Pathfinder Home Ent	France	33
Tomorrow Never Dies	1997	MGM	Germany	79
Topaz	1969	Universal	Scandinavia	134
Topkapi	1964	MGM	Turkey	89
Torn Curtain	1966	Universal	Scandinavia	134
Trainspotting	1996	Miramax Home Ent	UK	105
Tycoon	2002	New Yorker Video	Russia	146
V for Vendetta	2006	Warner	Germany	74
Vampyr	1932	Criterion	Scandinavia	125
Willy Wonka and the Chocolate Factory	1971	Warner	Germany	80
Wings of Desire	1987	MGM	Germany	71
Wings of the Dove, The	1997	Miramax	Italy	59
Woman with the Small Dog, The	1960	Artkino Pictures	Russia	141
Wonderful World of the Brothers Grimm, The	1962	MGM	Germany	83
World is Not Enough, The	1999	MGM	Turkey	92

ABOUT MUSEYON GUIDES

Museyon: A Curated Guide to Your Obsessions is a guide book series that gives the curious subject a new and differently informed look at their interests. Based out of New York City with origins in Tokyo, Paris, and just about everywhere in between, Museyon is an independent publisher of quality information.

ABOUT OUR ILLUSTRATOR

 Jillian Tamaki is an illustrator from Calgary, Alberta who now lives in Brooklyn, NY. In addition to her myriad editorial illustrations for publications such as *Entertainment Weekly, The New York Times,* and *SPIN*, she is also an award-winning graphic novelist. Co-authored alongside her cousin Mariko Tamaki, *Skim* was released in March 2008 and received the Ignatz Award for Best Graphic Novel.

Most memorable film/travel experience: While driving around Iceland, we got snowed in at the very top of the island, in a city called Akureyri. To while away the time, we hit the local theatre which was playing the film *Stardust*, part of which happened to be filmed in Iceland. The mossy green hills were instantly recognizable and the people in the theatre were quite amused, pointing and chuckling. It was very strange to be in a movie theatre near the Arctic Circle, and even stranger to see the landscape we'd been moving through for the last week up on the screen.

ACKNOWLEDGEMENTS

Photography for the Museyon Guides has been graciously provided by dozens of citizen photographers found through Flickr.com. Museyon would like to thank them, and all the companies and photo libraries below:

Photo Editor/Contributor: Michael Kuhle

Akira Chiba: 48, 62, 64, 66

flickr: 12, 14, 18, 21, 25, 26, 28, 30, 52, 63, 70, 72, 72, 76, 77, 82, 83, 100, 102, 104, 104, 109, 116, 122, 124, 125, 126, 129, 134, 135, 136, 137, 149, 155

istockphoto: 10, 36, 39, 40, 45, 46, 50, 58, 70, 72, 78, 94, 106, 116, 118, 119, 130, 132, 136, 140, 154

shutterstock: 16, 19, 22, 26, 32, 34, 34, 40, 42, 52, 54, 57, 60, 68, 72, 74, 76, 80, 84, 86, 87, 88, 88, 90, 96, 98, 110, 112, 120, 124, 138, 142, 144, 147, 147, 148, 152

Deniz Tavmen: 92, 99

Hotel Atlantic Kempinski Hamburg: 79

Everett Collection: 11, 16, 25, 33, 38, 47, 51, 59, 65, 89, 92, 105, 108, 117, 125, 128, 131, 141, 143

Every effort has been made to trace and compensate copyright holders, and we apologize in advance for any accidental omissions. We would be happy to apply the corrections in the following edition of this publication.